PRESIDENTIAL ELECTIONS

★ ★ ★ ★ ★ ★ ★ ★ ★ ★ ★ ★

PRESIDENTIAL ELECTIONS

*From Abraham Lincoln
to Franklin D. Roosevelt*

BY CORTEZ A. M. EWING

NORMAN : UNIVERSITY OF OKLAHOMA PRESS : 1940

★ ★ ★ ★ ★ ★ ★ ★ ★ ★ ★ ★

324.73
E95p

May 19, 1998
Sh. Gert.

COPYRIGHT 1940 BY THE UNIVERSITY OF OKLAHOMA PRESS. ALL RIGHTS RESERVED.
SET UP AND PRINTED AT NORMAN, OKLAHOMA, U.S.A, BY THE UNIVERSITY OF OKLA-
HOMA PRESS, PUBLISHING DIVISION OF THE UNIVERSITY. FIRST EDITION, 1940

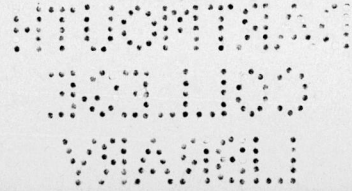

To My Parents

★ ★ ★ ★ ★

Preface

★ ★ ★ ★ ★ ★ ★ ★

THIS study is not a history of American political parties since the Civil War. Rather, the purpose is to attempt an interpretation of the more fundamental development of theories which have lain behind and beneath American politics. In implementing this purpose, attention has been focused upon the general results of elections rather than upon specific programs of the political parties.

What is the rôle of minor parties in our American political system? This and many other questions must challenge those who seek an understanding of the factors that move beneath the surface of American political campaigns. A mere study of the platforms offered to the voters reveals too little difference between major parties to justify any crisp generalizations concerning the reasons for Republican or Democratic success. The real motivating factors that turn whole sections against the party in power are too subtle, too elusive, to be attributed to any formal declarations. There are nuances, ephemeral and perhaps only subconsciously felt, that produce wholesale switches from one party to another.

In a democracy, there is a decision-making power that defies analysis. We speak of the electoral decision, of popular sovereignty, and of consent of the governed, with an abiding reverence. These are some of the perfumed phrases of our political polemics. But where does that decision-making power lie in America? Is the citizen of Georgia, voting the Democratic ticket in a year of Republican landslide triumph, a factor in that decision? I have sought, through analysis of the voting statistics, to throw some light upon this elusive phenomenon.

And finally, the technique of dividing the United States into sections is used for interpretative clarification. The sections set up in this study are not strictly geographical, economic, social, or racial; they are essentially political. Despite many apparent inconsistencies, the classification of states into East, Border, South, Middle West, and West is, I believe, justified by the fundamental generalizations of the study.

No one could reasonably claim more than relative accuracy in the breaking down of more than three hundred thirty-five million votes into state, party, section, and individual election categories. However, when that astronomical vote total was brought together from the many thousand separate entries, the resulting amount represented a deviation from the Curtis—*World Almanac* figure of less than one-tenth of one per cent. The voting statistics from 1864 to 1892 were taken from Francis Curtis; those from 1896 to 1936 were from the *World Almanac*.

I am indebted to my colleagues L. A. Doran and R. J. Dangerfield for many valuable suggestions and corrections that resulted from their critical reading of the manuscript, and to Mr. Frank Morris, who prepared the graphs. And my thanks and deep appreciation go to Miss June Tompkins

PREFACE

who, in the preparation of the manuscript, demonstrated again her uncanny ability to translate accurately the worst of hieroglyphics.

CORTEZ A. M. EWING

Norman, August 1, 1940.

Contents

PREFACE   vii
INTRODUCTION: DEMOCRATIC FOUNDATIONS   1
   I. THE BATTLE FOR BALLOTS   14
  II. SECTIONALISM PREFERRED   45
 III. THE MINOR PARTY MISSION   108
  IV. THE ELECTORAL COLLEGE   136
   V. GEOGRAPHY OF DECISION   189
  VI. AN INTERPRETATION   215
INDEX   219

TABLES

1. EFFECT OF THE 1896 ELECTION ON THE EAST'S PARTY ALLEGIANCES   50
2. THE RISE OF DEMOCRATIC STRENGTH IN THE EAST: 1920-1936   53

3. Comparison of the South's Republican Totals: 1924-1932 .... 70, 71
4. The Middle West and the Election of 1896 76
5. Internecine Democratic Struggle in the Middle West: 1896-1908 78
6. Democratic Upsurge in the Middle West: 1920-1936 86
7. Republican Percentages of Popular Votes: by States 104
8. Democratic Percentages of Popular Votes: by States 105
9. Agrarian Party Votes: by Sections 113
10. Prohibition Party Votes: by Sections 119
11. Socialist Percentages of Popular Votes: by States 124
12. State Percentages of Total Votes Cast for Minor Parties 128
13. Party Percentage Deviations from Absolute Electoral College Quotients 144
14. Sectional Aspects of Electoral Votes: 1864-1936 150
15. Five-Per-Cent-Plurality Elections: by Years and Sections 152
16. Party Winners of Ten-Per-Cent Elections: by Sections 160

CONTENTS

17. SECTIONAL EFFECTIVENESS IN THE ELECTORAL COLLEGE — 168
18. STATE ELECTORAL COLLEGE EFFECTIVENESS — 175
19. WASTED POPULAR VOTES: BY PERIODS, PARTIES, AND SECTIONS — 178, 179
20. SECTIONAL WASTAGE RECORDS AND NATIONAL AVERAGES — 187
21. POPULAR VOTES PER THOUSAND POPULATION — 199
22. VOTER PARTICIPATION: BY STATES AND PERIODS — 206, 207
23. AVERAGE EFFECTIVENESS OF POPULAR VOTES: BY STATES — 212

FIGURES

1. TOTAL POPULAR VOTES: BY PARTIES — 16
2. PERCENTAGE POPULAR VOTES: BY PARTIES — 43
3. SECTIONAL PERCENTAGES OF REPUBLICAN VOTE — 48
4. SECTIONAL PERCENTAGES OF DEMOCRATIC VOTE — 51
5. ELECTORAL COLLEGE VOTES: BY PARTIES — 138
6. POPULAR VOTES PER ELECTORAL VOTE: BY PARTIES — 140
7. SECTIONAL PERCENTAGES OF NATIONAL VOTE EFFECTIVENESS — 170
8. POPULATION AND POPULAR VOTES — 195
9. VOTES PER THOUSAND INHABITANTS: BY SECTIONS — 200
10. SECTIONAL PERCENTAGES OF AVERAGE NATIONAL VOTER PARTICIPATION — 210

★ ★ ★ ★ ★

INTRODUCTION

Democratic Foundations

★ ★ ★ ★ ★ ★ ★ ★

THE political history of the United States may be roughly divided into two periods separated by the Civil War. In the first, political conflict centered about the distribution of power in the American governmental system. Attention was focused primarily upon the Constitution. "It was the custom of many of the gentlemen of South Carolina," wrote Gaillard Hunt, "to carry about with them pocket-editions of the Constitution, and some of them knew it by heart."[1] Looking back over the shoulders of time, one is tempted to panegyrize the achievements of this first period. But it must be remembered that the citizens then living were probably no more perspicacious than those of today, and that they had not the perspective of the present to help them with their problems. They argued over strict and liberal interpretations of the Constitution, over the relation of the central government to the states, over fiscal policy, tariffs, internal improvements, and the disposition of the public domain.

The pens of historians are altogether impotent media for depicting the storm of bitterness that engulfed whole sec-

[1] *John C. Calhoun* (Philadelphia: Jacobs & Company, 1908) 290.

tions of this country in opposition to the then revolutionary doctrines of Jefferson, Jackson, and others of the so-called democratic school. Nevertheless, out of this political welter emerged the essential principles of American individualistic democracy. By the fourth decade of the nineteenth century, the principle of equality of all white citizens was generally accepted. De Tocqueville, the best of the foreign observers who came to criticize the United States, marveled at this acceptance and could not refrain from contrasting the conditions of these transplanted Europeans with those of their contemporary cousins in Europe.

In this march of democratic principle, no factor was more important than that of the public domain. Almost endless stretches of potentially rich agricultural land invited settlement by those with the energy and the will to create, for themselves, the fact of independence. The influence of this country's land policy in the growth of American agrarian democracy can scarcely be overestimated. Not only was the right to own his instruments of economic production legally presumed for the common man, but the fulfillment of that right was not too difficult of achievement. The eagerness with which Americans took advantage of this land policy may have resulted from the "Tory land hunger" of the time. Derived from English forbears, most Americans regarded land ownership as the means by which they could increase their self-importance and achieve social respectability. The result of this rush, however, was essentially the creation of bases for, and the principles of, American agrarian democracy, emblazoned on the shield of which were the great catchwords of American politics — liberty, equality, and individualism.

DEMOCRATIC FOUNDATIONS

The Civil War, marking the end of this first period, may reasonably be interpreted as arising in the challenge flung out by the new agrarian democracy. By the fortuity of colonization policy and the caprice of economics, a large section of the United States, the South, lay outside the stream of this democratic development. This does not mean that the South was wholly a section of large plantations and slave labor. The entire section, but especially Virginia, North Carolina, and Tennessee, utilized both the free and the slave systems of political economy. But where cotton, tobacco, and rice were the major agricultural commodities, the slavery forces dominated the politics of the state.

There is no need at this point to attempt an evaluation of the two systems. To do so would take one far into the antagonisms that surround the present-day issue of collectivism versus small-farm economy. From 1840 to 1860 geography decided the issue between them. The lands available for the three plantation crops were far less extensive than those suited to the production of wheat, corn, and livestock. Even from the South, ambitious settlers poured into the upper Missisippi Valley. The agrarian-democracy sections grew at a much faster pace than the plantation-slavery section. The challenge as expressed by Lincoln was: America cannot exist half-slave and half-free!

There may be legitimate doubt that the Lincoln apothegm was not, *per se*, an emotional political rallying cry. Why could not the United States have continued to exist under the constitution of 1855? Legally, it might have so remained, but politically, with triumphant equalitarian democracy on the march, the situation was almost intolerable. The defenders of slavocracy pleaded to the Constitution; their opponents pleaded to the immutability of natural law. The former relied upon a cold and almost lifeless document, a document that signified the area of agreement in a period when equalitarian democracy was in its swaddling clothes. But the eyes of the opponents of slavery were fixed upon a new objective which held for them the bewitching grandeur of a glorious dream.

Most will now agree that the slave section erred in seeking too long to forestall a formal democratic decision. As a defense mechanism, its leaders tended to render sacred its economic order and rallied their supporters for a defense to the death. Under this technique, the Constitution, a human document, was no longer of any great value; therefore it was abandoned on secession from the Union. Agrarian democracy then moved to the support of the Constitution and thereby created a new and effective coalition between the traditionalists and the higher-law evangelists.

The crux came in the election of Lincoln. The insistent pressure of the libertarians had already wrecked the Whigs and created a new Republican party; and, of more importance, it had already rendered impotent the erstwhile dominant Democratic party. Prior to 1860, the latter had been the most vital factor for peace. In fact, if the Democrats had been able to reconcile the sectional differences in political program and presidential candidacy, Lincoln's national career might have been restricted to his short term in the lower house of Congress.

If the slavocracy had remained behind the Constitution, had stood upon its rights to compensation for pecuniary damages, and had freely accepted as within the legitimate province of political action the solution of the dominant

DEMOCRATIC FOUNDATIONS

agrarian group, the United States might have escaped both the terrible cost of the Civil War and the not unimportant price of the resulting peace. For memories of the war between the sections remained so long in the minds of the electorate as to preclude consideration of many pressing issues. In fact, if the United States had performed its governmental functions from 1865 to 1885, in the light of isolating and solving problems, the history of the last half-century might have been substantially different.

If the first seventy-five years of this country's national existence were spent in consolidating the constitutional system upon a broad democratic basis, the last seventy-five years have been devoted to an entirely different problem. Even before the Civil War, there were evidences of the turn which the industrial order was to take. Railroad corporations, which were especially active in the fifties, were to produce political grief in the seventies. Thus, at the very time the United States was removing constitutional impediments to its basic principle of free democracy, the industrial order was emerging. This order was to challenge that basic principle, and the people, speaking sometimes through government and more often through splinter parties and other *ad hoc* organizations, were to meet that challenge by laws, labor unions, boycotts, and pious resolutions.

During the last three-quarters of a century, the political-party history of the United States has been concerned little with the form, but much with the functions of government. The American people have labored over matters of regulating the railroads, other business corporations, Wall Street, child labor, and the multitudinous "rackets" that arise in, or on the fringes of, the business world. They have worried over "hard" and "soft" money, the gold standard, "sixteen-to-one," treasury notes, and Townsend plans. And, especially since Henry George came out of the West with the warnings of his *Progress and Poverty*, the common man has placed great store in individual economic security. It is scarcely fortuitous that the height of Henry George's popularity, the publication of Bellamy's *Looking Backward*, the passing of the agricultural frontier, the enactment of the Interstate Commerce Commission Act, and, through the superiority of the open furnace, the United States' exceeding Great Britain in steel production, occurred between 1887 and 1890.

The purpose of this study is to follow the popular decision, as far as possible, through the votes in presidential elections from 1864 to 1936. Of course, this is not the whole picture, and there is no intention here to presume that it is. A complete picture could come only from a multi-volumed history, covering especially the political, economic, and social developments, as well as the effects which law, education, and engineering science have had upon the political scene. Who would undertake such an ambitious task? Common sense and the limitations of knowledge are now practically certain to restrict serious interpretations of this enigmatic period of American life to the shorter and more feasible treatment.

Any consideration of the political-party decisions must, of necessity, be viewed as only a part of the political story. The history of legislation and of administration is clearly outside, and the American people have discovered that, at best, there is many a slip between the cup and the lip, many an inconsistency between the votes in political elections and those in legislative chambers. The attempt here can be no more than the presentation of a general picture of the clash of political parties, out of which will naturally emerge a fairly accurate understanding of the real character of a political party. There are those who seek to interpret the program of this or that party as the natural evolution of the original principles upon which it was founded. Likewise, competing parties often claim to be intellectual descendants of one man. Thus, Washington and Jefferson are claimed by both the Republicans and the Democrats, as well as by practically all the minor parties. Once the particular property of the Republicans, Lincoln is now becoming a Democratic saint.

The truth of the matter is that the contributions of great leaders become the common heritage of the whole people. The Republicans could no more win an election if they stood openly against the political integrity of the common man than could the Democrats if they advocated the reinstitution of human slavery. A political party, therefore, is only a voluntary organization of voters, bound together by more or less common principles, and operating with the avowed intention of winning control of the government. The party platform is pieced together so as to receive the greatest possible electoral support in present and future elections. Parties consequently gamble on the turn of history; sometimes they miss and pass into the limbo of good intentions. The trail of American political history is lined with the bleached skeletons of parties that missed the turn.

Major parties seldom risk destruction for the mere chance of being right with future history; the stakes are too high. They, therefore, lay a course fairly close to public opinion. This lack of confidence in clairvoyance is not to be regarded as unworthy of them, for major parties must operate in the living present and not in some idealized future circumstance. They must propose programs for living persons. As a result, American major parties find themselves in practical agreement upon the important issues. The campaigns become, under those conditions, mere popularity contests for the rival candidates.

Opposition parties have an advantage in program building; they can attack governmental policy on specific grounds. The opposition party, therefore, is usually the one which stresses the protection of individual rights and human liberty. The governing party must take the responsibility which accompanies its position. In implementing that responsibility, it must enact legislation that seeks the balance between the public welfare and individual liberty. Naturally, such regulation produces its martyrs, who may be defended by the opposition. For this reason, many observers have characterized the Democratic party as the champion of liberty since the Civil War. Probably it has been, but it must also be remembered that it has not had to take much responsibility for governing during that long period.

That this study is by no means the complete party story is readily agreed, for it omits the entire congressional facet of our national parties. That must remain a serious defect. However, like by-elections, the off-year congressional elections have, on many occasions, been clearly contradictory to the general trend. At other times, they may well have initiated important changes in party fortunes, but they have been excluded from the present study because of the desire to present as simple and uncomplicated a picture as possible.

To facilitate an understanding of the clash of parties in the last nineteen elections, in this study the United States has been divided into five major sections. The division is purely arbitrary. No two scholars would freely agree upon any one sectional demarcation; the national picture is far too complex for that. The politics of most states is, *per se*, almost as complicated as that of the United States. The sectionalization cannot be achieved upon economic criteria, for states like Indiana and Ohio defy such classification. Social standards offer no more assistance than does habitual linguistic error or prevalence of the broad "a" in the common language of the people. The length of time in the Union is of no importance at all in determining political alignments, for in the last nineteen elections Vermont has never gone Democratic, and Georgia has never gone Republican.

The possibilities for classification of the forty-eight states into regions, sections, and sub-sections are practically unlimited. One could, by generous definition, easily boost the number to more than a hundred. To make so many divisions would be no more helpful than to consider the forty-eight states as a single unity. Professor Holcomb employed twelve sections in his splendid analysis, but the interrelations among twelve sections must inevitably produce a very involved political story. Thus, while ackowledging the existence of many telling objections to the present classification, the author has divided the states into sections designated as the East, Border, South, Middle West, and West.

The East includes the six New England states and New York, New Jersey, and Pennsylvania. There may be important reasons for including Ohio in this section, especially since she has become so vital as a manufacturing area, but she is also distinctly middle western. Many would include

Delaware and Maryland in the East, and some would also place West Virginia alongside Pennsylvania because of their mutual interests in coal production. But all three of these states were below the historic Mason and Dixon's Line, and in the political mores, there exist more similarities with the upper-tier states of the South than with the states of the East.

Delaware, Maryland, West Virginia, Kentucky, and Missouri have been placed in the Border. All were within the slavery section prior to 1860, but none followed the eleven southern states out of the Union. All presented, in the Reconstruction era, preponderant Democratic majorities. In a very real sense, these were the traditional buffer states between the North and the South, though it should be noted that West Virginia was not brought into the Union as a separate state until during the Civil War. For the most part, there exists in them a small-holding agricultural economy, which tends toward independence in politics, and since the turn of the century these states have moved into the doubtful class. Many scholars would place Missouri in the Middle West, but she really resembles none of the middle western states in political behavior. She cannot go with the South on account of the strong and continuous Republican tradition. Kentucky could much more plausibly be regarded as southern. Diversification of agriculture plus the inferior position of plantation economy in Virginia, North Carolina, Tennessee, and Kentucky offers a real basis for the creation of another section, but to do so would leave Missouri noncontiguous with other Border states. Thus, though strongly attached to the traditional Democratic party, and only

DEMOCRATIC FOUNDATIONS

scarcely less so than the other three states of the upper South, Kentucky is included in the Border classification.

The South gives less trouble than the other sections; it is the South of history. Only Oklahoma is added to the Confederacy of 1861; had she been in existence at that time there is little doubt that she would have become the twelfth member. Most of her population springs from southern heritage and, though other industries have challenged it for leadership, the production of cotton remains one of the main agricultural occupations of her people. With the exception of the three tobacco and textile states—Virginia, North Carolina, and Tennessee—the whole section is permeated with the psychology of cotton economy. This psychology appears to have some mysterious connection with an almost unfailing preference for the Democratic party. None of the sections has such a record of party regularity as has the South.

The Middle West is a resuscitation of the old Northwest Territory, now comprising seven states. The induction of new states to the west of Iowa and Minnesota breathed confusion into the meaning of Northwest. There are those who maintain that the Middle West extends from Pittsburgh to the Rocky Mountains, reaching far enough south to steal Oklahoma from the South. The arbitrariness in excluding those immediate western neighbors of Iowa and Minnesota from the Middle West has a logical basis. It is true that eastern Kansas and eastern Nebraska are not greatly different from neighboring Iowa in economy or even in political thinking, but the semi-arid and red lands to the west of those corn-belt prairies are too distinctly western to be included in the Middle West. There is another factor: the seven states of this section were all in the Union during the Civil War, and that fact dominated their politics for years to come. For instance, they were too much crystallized politically to be swept from their feet by the Bryan campaign of 1896, a fact which was not true of the next tier of states to the west.

The West comprises the remaining fifteen states. They are the West, and geographically there can be no objection to this classification. Politically, they have revealed an independence of the other sections that is truly amazing. Even the breaks in party fortune have shown a remarkable consistency throughout the region. In fact, no analyst can today ignore it, for the decisiveness with which it has plumped its electoral votes since 1916 makes the West more important than sections which do not present a solid front. Not since the re-election of Wilson has the section lost an electoral vote! Moreover, this combination of wheat-belt, mineral empire, and Pacific littoral exerts an influence in national affairs far in excess of that to which it is entitled by population criteria. Being in almost colonial relationship to the financial centers of the nation, the West has developed an effective technique of political bargaining. The great irrigation and power dams that dot its landscape are evidence of this political cleverness.

The vote totals from which the graphs in this study were constructed were drawn from four main sources. Unfortunately, disparities exist among the so-called authentic figures. For the earlier part of the period, there will probably never be authoritative data; from 1880 to the present, there is less disagreement. However, when one starts from the votes of individual states, the totals are sometimes at variance with those of other compilers. The disparities apparently result from failure to count minor-party votes, from rejection of "write-in" and other such irregular votes, and from the erroneous inclusion of mutilated ballots. Also, carelessness on the part of some compilers makes necessary the checking of sources against one another. For instance, the total vote given for a state may correspond with that of another compilation, but the party totals may be switched. Or, one may give only the totals of the two major parties. In other counts the totals may be correct, but the year designations may be interchanged. Therefore, regardless of the care taken to prevent error, one cannot reasonably pretend to have completed an absolutely accurate compilation of voting statistics.

For the period from 1860 to 1900, the author has used principally the Stanwood[2] and Curtis[3] accounts for national totals, and the *Whig Almanac*, the *Annual Cyclopaedia*, Peter Cooper's *National Politics*, and older editions of the *World Almanac* for the state totals. The last source is fairly accurate for the state totals since 1896, except for the minor-party and scattering votes. These latter were assembled from Professor Robinson's excellent compilation.[4]

[2] Edward Stanwood, *A History of the Presidency* (Boston: Houghton Mifflin, 1916), 2 vols.
[3] Francis Curtis, *The Republican Party* (New York: G. P. Putnam's Sons, 1904), 2 vols.
[4] Edgar Eugene Robinson, *The Presidential Vote 1896-1932* (Stanford: Stanford University Press, 1934).

CHAPTER ONE

The Battle for Ballots

IN the last nineteen presidential elections, from 1864 to 1936, more than three hundred and thirty-five million ballots were marked for presidential electors. The individual totals rose from the four million of 1864 to the more than forty-five million votes in 1936. During that period, when the United States was maturing economically at an amazing pace, every election except one (1904) posted a ballot increase over its immediate predecessor, though at times the accretion was not large, and at others, the ratio of adult participation perceptibly declined. As will be apparent later in this study, the 1880 adult-participation mark was not surpassed until after the adoption of the woman-suffrage amendment to the Constitution.

Of those nineteen elections, the Democrats have won but six. From 1864 to 1928, the Republicans won thirteen of the seventeen contests. Thus the Democrats occupied a decidedly minority position. There were logical reasons for this lack of electoral success. The Civil War was a telling blow to Democratic respectability. Retreating behind their geographic frontiers in 1861, the southern Democrats had charged abolitionists and Republicans with treason to the

Constitution and to the inviolability of contract. As early as 1850, the southern Whigs had begun to cross political no-man's land to join the Democrats, who thereby became the avowed champions of slavery, and later, of the right of secession. Simultaneously, the reverse process was consummated in the North. Peace-loving, and therefore compromising Democrats were forced, by the popular demands of their constituents, to oppose slavery. The inevitable result of this grass-roots ultimatum was the accelerated growth of the new Republican party. After the opening of hostilities, northern Democrats who remained loyal to the Union found it increasingly difficult to defend their party. Democracy, with a capital "D," was regarded as synonymous with rebellion and therefore entirely antithetical to democracy, in the lower case. The opprobrium was to remain until Republican administrations, careless and sometimes arrogant, violated ethical rules and principles that were sacred to the followers of equalitarian agrarianism.

The seventy-two years covered in this study may logically be divided into four periods. The first, from 1864 to 1876, witnessed four straight Republican triumphs. The second, from 1880 to 1892, found the Democrats beating back to split the four elections equally with their rivals. The third extended from 1896 to 1916; although the Democrats won both the 1912 and the 1916 contests, their success derived primarily from internecine Republican strife. The fourth, from 1920 to 1936, might be designated as the post-war period. The Republicans won the first three, and the Democrats the last two elections. Throughout these sixteen years, there was threat of party realignment. The country was sick economically, though the universal discontent subsequent to the stock market crash of 1929 induced most people to believe they had been reasonably comfortable in the nine preceding years.

The popular-vote angle of these presidential elections is shown in *Figure 1*. From 1864 to 1896 the two major parties were reasonably close in vote totals. There was considerable

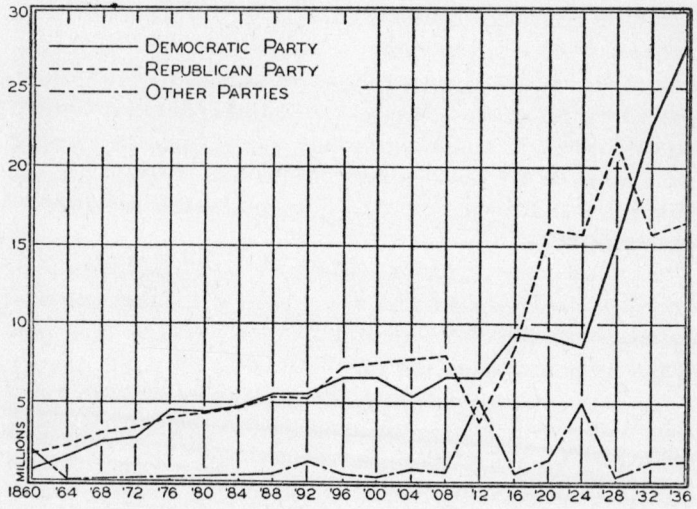

Figure 1.—Total Popular Votes: by Parties

fluctuation in the next five contests, followed by five more that produced a period of wild change of party fortunes, completely alien to the rather staid and dependable party habits of the sixty years preceding the end of the World War. Also, during the last two periods, the third-party totals are evidence of popular dissatisfaction with the programs and policies of the major parties. The fundamental interpretation of the graph is the loss of party regularity that has developed since the first World War. During the period before that cataclysm, which exerted such a tremendous influence upon the international order, the average American was born a Republican or a Democrat. It was a period of classic crystallization of party allegiance. Party leaders dramatized this fidelity of their liege men by recounting the unwitting errors of their childhood; according to the stories, the Republican adolescent had inadvertently uttered the word "Democrat," whereupon his mother, faithful to the higher ideals of America, has rinsed his mouth with soapy water. The Democratic story retained the penalty but substituted "Republican" or "Lincoln" as evidence of the violation of the principle of human decency.

Since 1920 such campaign techniques have been ineffectual. Appeal is made to emotions, but tradition has lost much of its hypnotic effect as a determinant of political behavior. American politics may still be discussed in the nomenclature of tradition, but an increasingly large number of voters, who align themselves for or against a party program, are now motivated by a new perfumed phrase—standard of living! Emerging almost imperceptibly from the philosophy of agrarian democracy, it expressed the common citizen's insistence upon individual integrity and independence in a world that presented the challenge of finance capitalism and its amazing concentrations of economic power. Thus, the popular stampede to Herbert Hoover in 1928, is attributable in part to the faith which voters had in him, the reputedly capable "social engineer." He would protect the common people from the financial goblins! When he failed, at least in the popular mind, those seeking the goal of economic security turned blithely and without equivocation to Franklin D. Roosevelt. And when they were convinced that he understood the historic task which was his, they swarmed in even greater numbers to his standard in 1936.

The switching of party allegiance was the exception rather than the rule before 1920 and especially before 1896. In the early period, "turn-coat" and "apostate" were powerful verbal weapons in the repertoire of political campaigners. The politicians of this era were not stupid; they employed techniques and phrases that brought favorable responses from the voters. People generally had little respect for those who abandoned their parties. The Civil War, which had divided the country, many communities, and even unnumbered families, was still fresh in the minds of the people. Loyalty was therefore a medal of honor, and respect was accorded, though perhaps grudgingly, even to the loyal members of the "wrong" party. The error was one of judgment, but mistakes of the head were never so despicable as mistakes of the heart!

A modern Rip Van Winkle, returning to the political scene after a forty-year absence, would in 1932 have had cause to wonder at the strange order of things. Men like Harold Ickes, Henry Wallace, George Norris, and William Woodin, all nominal Republicans, were excoriating the formal Republican candidate and advocating the election of a Democrat. This was no Mugwump uprising, which would have been, in comparison, a mere parlor revolt. If this modern Rip had gone down into the constituencies, he would have found cause for even greater consternation. Millions of 1928 Hoover supporters were cheering for his opponent. No one was branding them with apostasy. Any such allusion would probably have increased the tide against the Republican ticket.

The Reconstruction Era, 1864-1876

The Republicans won each of the four national elections during this period, though their popular-vote total of 1876 was exceeded by that of the Democrats. In the first contest (1864), with Lincoln seeking re-election upon the platform of successful prosecution of the war, the Republicans dropped their official title and called themselves the Union party. The intention was to achieve a coalition of all those who supported the war policy.[1] The Democrats chose General George B. McClellan as presidential candidate, but he received only 45 per cent of the national canvass. Lincoln carried twenty-two of the twenty-five states, losing only Delaware, Kentucky, and New Jersey.[2]

Under the nominal leadership of General U. S. Grant, the Republicans won both the 1868 and the 1872 elections. Governor Horatio Seymour was the losing Democratic candidate in 1868. The party had no official leader in the next election. In general, party members supported the candidacy of Horace Greeley, who headed the Liberal Republican ticket. The high-handed methods of the Radical Republican leaders alienated many members of the regular Republican party. Thus the doughty editor's candidacy was inspired by northern reaction to the treatment of southern people.

[1] The Democrats favored a program of terminating hostilities at the earliest possible moment and deplored interference by the national government with the constitutional rights of citizens.

[2] Only in Kentucky did McClellan have a decisive advantage, the vote there being 67,124 to 28,980. In Delaware and New Jersey, Lincoln received 47.3 per cent of the votes.

The two elections fell in the trough of the Reconstruction era. Thousands of southern whites were disfranchised for their part in the war. Many southern states were governed by northern-inspired régimes, whose record is very spotted. No period in American history has challenged the interest of historians and special investigators more than this, but the literary picture is still very much muddled. There are such anomalies as "northern" histories and "southern" histories, unnatural offspring in the genealogy of a respectable literary family. "Scalawags," "carpetbaggers," "Black Republicans," "libertines," "rapists," "highbinders," "adventurers," and "buccaneers" parade through the pages of the southern histories, resulting in the creation of a continuing sectional feeling against what southerners regarded as the period of an alien plunderage. In northern histories, the missionary Reconstructionists, intent upon spreading the light of Christianity and democracy, are presented as men worthy of much praise; as a result, these accounts refer to those same characters as "reformers," "altruists," "true democrats," "equalitarians," "Christian gentlemen," "patriots," and "courageous and self-sacrificing representatives of the true American spirit."

The Republican 1868 and 1872 percentages of the popular vote were 52.6 per cent and 55.6 per cent, respectively. Both of Grant's administrations were brought into being by popular majorities. With saner congressional leadership and better presidential advice, the party might well have maintained that high position in the popular esteem for twenty years, or until the disappearance of free land for enterprising husbandmen and until war memories ceased to be quickening political stimuli. The supreme error of the

Republican leadership was that it failed to implement the hopes and aspirations of agrarian democracy. Through intimate and sometimes corrupt support of the new industrialism, which at many points was antithetical to agrarian interests, the party's agricultural membership dwindled rapidly during the financial panic of 1873. And the Democrats, moving from their insignificant position of 1872, when they had no Democratic candidate for the presidency, found themselves the champion of many embattled farmers and mechanics. Agrarians especially feared the concentration of economic power, and Jay Cooke, suave manipulator of shady financial transactions, came to epitomize this new threat to equalitarian individualism. Railroad corporations and the distillery cartel were the whipping posts of rural constituencies. And when they nominated the esteemed Samuel Tilden, of New York, the Democrats were in position to challenge the Republicans for the first time since the South had sought to break the constitutional bonds of union.

The election of 1876 was one of the most important in the national history of this country. For the first time since 1860, all states participated.[3] Except for South Carolina, Florida, and Louisiana, the South had freed itself from its Reconstruction masters. The number of voters was increased by removal of disqualifications against southern whites; and the bars had not yet been raised against southern Negroes. Moreover, the acknowledged integrity and ability of Rutherford B. Hayes, Republican candidate, were not sufficient to overcome the apostasy of thousands of erstwhile Republican supporters.

There was no official popular-vote count for the 1876

[3] Electors were appointed by legislatures in Colorado, Florida, and Louisiana.

election, and there was considerable difference between the totals announced by the two parties.[4] Nevertheless, the election, with its contested electoral college quotas, was so close and confused that the Electoral Commission of 1877 was created to determine the winner. After questionable decisions of the commission, all upon a strictly partisan basis, Hayes was declared the winner by the margin of a single vote.[5]

In party-vote totals for this first period, the Republicans' 52.1 per cent was safely ahead of the Democratic mark of 47.3 per cent.[6] The period is anomalous, in that war and the bitterness which it generated dominated the national political scene. "Waving the bloody shirt" was effective technique in the first three campaigns.

The "Fifty-Fifty" Period

The second period (1880-1892) saw the two major parties fight four elections on even terms. Each won two, but in none of the four contests did the winning party poll a majority of the popular vote. The protest tide reached its peak

[4] The two counts, as given in Curtis, *op. cit.*, II, 64, were: Democratic Count: Democrats 4,300,590; Republicans 4,036,298; others, 81,737. Republican Count: Democrats 4,033,768; Republicans 4,285,992; others, 81,737.

[5] See Paul L. Haworth, *The Hayes-Tilden Election of 1876* (Cleveland: Burrows Bros., 1906) xi, 365.

[6] The following table gives the figures for the four periods. The 1876 Democratic count was used in the compilation for the first period.

Period	Republican	Democrat	Others	Total
1864-76	12,789,570	11,612,777	134,945	24,537,292
1880-92	19,939,047	20,212,483	2,185,604	42,337,134
1896-16	41,597,077	39,728,898	7,708,469	89,034,444
1920-36	86,007,117	82,693,761	8,899,260	177,600,138

in the final election (1892), when the newly formed Populist party received more than a million and a quarter votes— a veritable threat to the continuance of the two-party system!

On the rising tide of popularity in 1876, the Democrats anticipated national triumph four years later. The congressional elections of 1878 further improved the party's morale, but their enthusiasm launched too many investigatory adventures in Congress. This hypercritical policy caused a reaction in favor of the Republicans, and when the latter nominated the respected James A. Garfield, the party's rank and file were sufficiently increased to give Garfield a slight plurality over General Hancock, the Democratic nominee. General James B. Weaver, the Greenback candidate, polled more than three hundred thousand votes, or thirty times Garfield's small popular plurality.

In 1884 the Democrats elected their first president since the unfortunate Buchanan. Chester A. Arthur, who succeeded the assassinated Garfield in 1881, was apparently more interested in patronage than in corrective national legislation. Thus, for three years, the Republicans languished for lack of dynamic leadership. On the other hand, Grover Cleveland had earned a reputation as reform governor of New York. His candidacy was further strengthened by the revolt of the Mugwumps, rebellious intellectuals headed by Carl Schurz, Henry Ward Beecher, and George William Curtis. Cleveland's plurality in New York was but 1,149 votes in a total canvass of 1,167,169. The New York decision gave the Democrats a majority in the electoral college. The Democratic national plurality was but 23,005 of a total vote of 10,052,706. Moreover, the Greenback and Prohibition parties received a total vote fourteen times this small Democratic plurality.

Seeking re-election in 1888, Cleveland again won a small plurality—100,476 votes—only to lose through the vagaries of electoral college decision. Benjamin Harrison, the Republican, carried New York by thirteen thousand, giving him his necessary electoral college majority. Minor parties polled almost four hundred thousand votes, and thus, for the third consecutive time, the president was a minority choice.

The fourth consecutive minority-choice election followed in 1892. Cleveland and Harrison were again the nominees, and the 1888 decision was reversed. Cleveland increased his plurality to 380,961 votes, but the minor parties polled more than one and one-quarter million votes. For the first time since 1860, minor parties threatened the hegemony of the two-party system. In 1892 their canvass amounted to almost 11 per cent of the total vote. Thus, the fact of primary importance in this election was not that Cleveland was elected, but that the protest vote had become so large as to make necessary a reorganization of national parties. That realignment was attempted in the next campaign with results disastrous to the party which sought to merge the protesters into its rank and file.

Rampant Republicanism, 1896-1916

In the interpretation of periods of national politics, there exists always the temptation to label them as of a particular intellectual vintage. Thus, the Reconstruction era was one in which the dominant party asserted its moral right to educate white southerners in the theology of democratic equalitarianism, patriotism, and Americanism. The second period exhibited a tremendous popular faith in an ever-expanding America and in the achievement of the general good through the agency of enlightened self-interest. Grover Cleveland epitomized this philosophy. The citizens, he said, should support the government instead of the government's supporting the citizens. According to the formula of Cleveland, Godkin, Schurz, and other leaders of this Utilitarian era, the public welfare was not a fortuitous circumstance; it was a collective condition inevitably flowing from individual triumph over nature and fellow man.

But what of those who fared ill in this continuous and merciless struggle? In an agrarian society, the differences in individual income were not so great as to produce powerful political blocs of the envious and defeated. The rise of corporate America, with its ostentatious display of wealth and its utter disregard for the feelings of agrarian democracy, was sufficient to generate this common feeling of envy in whole classes of people. Farmers were the first to resent the plain implications of corporate industrialism. The environmental prerequisite to a fruition of Jeffersonian agrarianism, never universal in America, was challenged by this new order, an order based upon pay rolls, monopoly prices, and political tampering. The agrarian idea of democracy embraced an ever-expanding freedom and an increased economic independence. Its farmer adherents naturally regarded this new order of corporatism as only a recrudescence of the system of privilege against which they had battled from the beginning of United States history. Agrarians, in fact reacted vociferously against Andrew Carnegie's "Gospel of Wealth."

Corporate capitalism was, in agrarian eyes, erasing the opportunity for equalitarian democracy. But how should this new danger be combatted? It thrived in the *milieu* of open competition, which was the *sine qua non* of the individualistic system. To meet it by governmental intervention was to utilize a technique antithetical to the individualism which was threatened by corporate capitalism. Nevertheless, the agrarians reasoned that the costs of non-intervention were greater than those which resulted from their philosophic inconsistency. And in making this decision, the government was brought into the economic order as a cleansing, purifying instrument, to restrain those whose impersonal organizations and techniques were operating against the very opportunity for personal equality. The interventionist point of view was put forth in the programs of the Greenback, the Anti-monopoly, the Prohibition, and the Populist parties, as well as in the avowed principles of economic and social organizations such as the Knights of Labor and the United Labor party. As corporate capitalism continued to prosper, the volume of protest correspondingly increased.

The amazing Populist poll of 1892 was a threat to both major parties, but especially to the Democrats. Under the leadership of "Tom" Watson, "Cyclone" Davis, "Stump" Ashby, and others of that school of political leaders, the hold of the Democrats upon the South was jeopardized. What if the Populists took over in this traditionally Democratic section? Such might prove fatal to the national Democratic party, for it would then have no safe political ground whose congressional representatives would keep the party alive in the lean years. In the past, even though Democrats had lost several consecutive national elections, they kept their organization alive with success in the safe Democratic states of the South.

There was another potent reason for the Democratic decision to fuse with the interventionist Populists. The Republicans were the traditional party of tariff protection and manufacturing interests were therefore preponderantly favorable to them. The Democrats were the party of the importers and of those who had to face the competition of larger manufacturing concerns. If the Republicans had adopted an interventionist attitude, with its incidental restrictions upon business, the party would have lost much of its financial support. By retaining the loyalty of this business element, the party was in position to withstand the rigors of national defeat.

The campaign of 1896 represents, therefore, a complete departure from political principles of almost constitutional importance. The Democrats fused with the Populists and assumed thereby the responsibility of regulating business in the event of national triumph. It should be noted here that this intervention did not imply nationalization of industrial property. Socialists were freaks in this decade, for their announced program was alien to American thinking and their numbers too insignificant to merit serious consideration. At best, the interventionists of 1896 had not pushed beyond the functional content of nineteenth century progressivism, which embodied the idea that the government should restrain the more successful so that others might have a better opportunity to get their shares. It was competition under definite rules of procedural ethics. The laws were merely to serve as rules of the game. Presumably play would be just as hard and as strenuous, but certain tactics were anathema to the concept of gentlemanly conduct.

Fusion with the Populists was, therefore, a compromise between high principles and practical politics. To save their position in the South, Democrats had to effect the compromise, but its consummation alienated many erstwhile faithful members. These latter had long believed that the tariff was obnoxious because it constituted an artificial interference with the natural circumstances of supply and demand. Compromise with avowed interventionists was, therefore, a signal that the Democratic party had abandoned its traditional principle. This freed the *laissez-faire* Democrats from their allegiance and thrust them into a position in which they could choose between the two great parties. Since neither was fundamentally sound, they could choose the relatively less objectionable, with the feeling that no permanent allegiance was involved in the choice.

The wholesale political realignment of 1896 ushered in a new era in American politics. McKinley's six hundred thousand plurality over William Jennings Bryan (and fusion) was the largest plurality since Grant's re-election in 1872. Yet Bryan's total was almost a million votes higher than any previous Democratic poll. The new alignment of voters reflected surprising sectional trends. For instance, the Democrats recovered their former preponderant position in the South and won a new respect in the West, but they lost in the East and Border sections. The industrial centers voted strongly against the unorthodox economics of the agrarian Bryan. Republican propaganda stampeded the workers to McKinley and the "full dinner-pail." Interestingly enough, this slogan was taken *in toto* from the political history of the

English free-trading party. The snubbing which it received by industrial labor reveals the essential agrarian character of the Bryan revolt.

The same major candidates faced each other in 1900, when the Republicans increased their plurality to almost eight hundred thousand votes. The total poll was only one hundred thousand above that of 1896. The threat of Bryan's agricultural radicalism was not enough to induce the old women of both sexes, as in 1896, to rush to the polls and save America from certain economic ruin. The adult-voting mark for 1900 was twenty-three per thousand less than in 1896.

Following this second consecutive defeat, the Democrats altered their party strategy. Though Bryan had proved himself to be one of the really great political leaders of American history, his defeats, narrow though they were, proved that the country was not yet ready for interventionism. Also upon replacing the assassinated McKinley, Theodore Roosevelt had shown a disposition to employ the strong arm of the national government to redress the wrongs of the common man. In other words, the Republicans had moved, partly at least, into the Democratic position. Consequently, conservative Democrats, as a matter of strategy, demanded that the party return to the pre-fusion stand on currency and individualism. Bryan stepped aside and Judge Alton B. Parker, of New York, contested the 1904 election with the dynamic Roosevelt.

The Democratic *volte face* resulted in party disaster. The Republican plurality leaped to more than two and one-half million votes. Only the South remained staunchly behind the party. Not one of the thirteen western states went Democratic. It was the worst Democratic defeat since

1872. Republican superiority, in this era of prosperity, was more pronounced than at any time since the Civil War. Following the rout of 1904, the Democrats burned their bridges behind them. The vote had proved beyond doubt that the people would no longer support the non-interventionist program, which, for strategic reasons, the Democrats had readopted for this particular election. The party turned almost unanimously to Bryan; and the Commoner made his third great race, this time against William Howard Taft. Though he boosted slightly his 1896 vote, the Republicans won by one and one-quarter million votes. However, Bryan added 1,324,615 votes, or 26 per cent to the Parker poll. Taft added but sixty thousand to the 1904 Republican total, and the minor party vote was practically the same—slightly over six hundred fifty thousand—in both elections.

Triumphant though they had been in the past four national elections, the rank and file of the Republicans were becoming increasingly critical of the platform and the administrative record of the party. Theodore Roosevelt had sensed the popular feeling against concentration of economic power, and though he had scorned the literary efforts of the Muckrakers, as he dubbed them, he nevertheless swaggeringly launched a great "trust-busting" campaign. Much to the disgust of business leaders, the populace enjoyed the Roman holidays that eventuated in the prosecution of the oil and tobacco trusts. When President Taft appeared little inclined to continue the entertainment, the interventionist Republicans, speaking through LaFollette, Norris, Cummins, and other Progressive leaders, threatened revolt if the party did not place itself unequivocally on the side of the common man.

The issue came to a crisis in the Republican convention of

THE BATTLE FOR BALLOTS

1912. Under the leadership of Theodore Roosevelt, the interventionists bolted the convention and proceeded to organize the Progressive (Bull Moose) party. Pledged generally to a liberal program, the Democrats nominated Woodrow Wilson. Taft was the natural choice of the conservative (Stand-Pat) Republicans. Not since 1896 had America witnessed so brilliant a political campaign. Though receiving less than 42 per cent of the total vote, Wilson was elected. Roosevelt was second with 27 per cent; Taft third with 23 per cent; and the Socialists, Prohibitionists, and Socialist Laborites fourth, with a collective total of 1,135,013 votes, or almost 8 per cent. Parties favoring some degree of governmental control accounted for over three-quarters of the fifteen million votes.

In sixteen short years the interventionists had increased in numbers until no party could afford to stand on the traditional *laissez-faire* platform. The first two years of Wilson's administration were featured by the enactment of important regulatory statutes, among which were the Clayton Act, the Federal Trade Commission Act, and the Federal Reserve Act. Indeed, the entire complexion of the national economy might have been altered but for the outbreak of the European war. The United States sensed the necessity of bolstering its defenses. Thereafter, further reform of the economic order was postponed and the campaign of 1916 was mainly concerned with the war issue. Wilson stood upon his record of having kept the country out of war; the Republicans charged that he had compromised the dignity of the United States by not protecting American life and property in the war zones and by muddling in our relations with Mexico. Wilson's popular plurality was almost six hundred thousand votes, which was 127,702 votes short of a majority.

In the six elections of this transitional period, the Republicans won the first four, the Democrats the final pair. Of the more than eighty-nine million popular votes, 46.7 per cent went to the Republicans, 44.6 per cent to the Democrats, and the remaining 9.6 per cent to minor parties. However, 53.5 per cent of the minor party total derived in the Progressive poll of 1912; and when the Socialist and Prohibitionist polls are added to that of the Progressives, the 1912 third-party contribution to the period's protest total rises to 65.2 per cent.

Morals, Intervention, and the Good Life, 1920-1936

The fourth, and contemporary, period in these eighty years of party history had an inauspicious beginning. Unlike 1864, 1880, and 1896, the year 1920 came as an anti-climax to events much more momentous—the war, the armistice, and the Treaty of Versailles. People were tired of politics—international, national, state, and local! They had contributed freely of money, blood, emotion, and constant attention. Even the debates on the world order proposed by Wilson failed to stir the American people as deeply as they would have under more sanguine circumstances, even as deeply as the debates on the repeal of the United States embargo did in late 1939.

As was pointed out above, the war occurred at a very inopportune moment for America. During 1913 and early 1914 the national administration had labored fruitfully in the enactment of reform measures long overdue. No doubt the remainder of Wilson's first administration would have produced fewer measures of first-rank importance, even if the war had not engaged Europe, for there appear to be definite limits to the amount of reform legislation that a people and its economic order can assimilate. Even if the country had rested until 1920, it might have had the will then to take up where it had left off in 1914.

The value of conjecture upon the point is nil, for the same political conditions will never again be presented to the American people. The war did come, and after almost three years of tight-rope walking, the United States fell into the maelstrom. Before the country could emerge its people were hyper-conscious of their idealism and of their rôle as protector of the civilized world. They had gone forth to save democracy and to provide, through example and advice, the mechanics of freedom to all mankind, even to some peoples who neither understood nor desired it. And in their excessive zeal they unconsciously developed in themselves an unworthy obscurantism. They could measure freedom by the Constitution and judge virtue by racial classification. Their feeling of self-importance led them into the danger of assuming that, as a modern "chosen people," they need have no fears concerning the permanency of their economic and social order, and any one who criticised it was viewed as an ungrateful soul who did not deserve the high privilege of enjoying it. The American people were, as Frank I. Cobb remarked, willing to die but not to think for their country.

The new feeling of self-importance found expression in numerous interferences with individual discretion. The Constitution was amended, prohibiting the manufacture, sale, and transportation of intoxicants. Censorships were imposed on books, plays, and "dangerous ideas." Before they had had an opportunity to present their arguments, articulate aliens were advised to "go back where they came from!" Extreme vigilance arose in the Ku Klux Klan, and local communities were purged of un-American ideas and sentiments through direct and illegal means. Minorities were the chief sufferers from these emotional outbursts. America had discovered its power; finding no ready victim, it indulged in self-flagellation. This new asceticism taught the new faith—faith in efficiency! The American people were willing worshippers at the altar of naked power!

In such a state of national psychology, the United States entered the Artificial Decade (1920-1929). After a deadlock in the Republican convention, revealing the inability of the party to nominate any one of the three leading candidates — Frank Lowden, Hiram Johnson, and General Leonard Wood—the gonfalon finally went to "dark-horse" Warren G. Harding, of Ohio, with Calvin Coolidge, of Massachusetts, as his running-mate. The Democrats chose Governor James Cox, of Ohio, and Franklin D. Roosevelt, of New York. Little need be said of the campaign. Though it was the first national election in which women could vote throughout the country there was little interest. Harding pleaded for a "return to normalcy," and Cox was no Wilson in arousing the common man.

The lethargic electorate warmed to the Republican appeal. Harding posed as an average American. He even smoked cigarettes, and took no pains to hide the fact. Later, the country learned that at the little house on K Street, he enjoyed a good brisk game of draw poker. Those who objected to Harding's personal habits did not have to leave the Republican premises, for Coolidge was the very personification of Puritan rectitude of conduct. And the Republicans were

THE BATTLE FOR BALLOTS

opposed to any further interference in European affairs. That alien tangle had been straightened out. The "normalcy" appeal received more than sixteen million votes, while Cox got but nine million. Minor parties accounted for one and one-half million.

Amid a wild storm of charges and counter-charges, President Harding died, and Coolidge became the executive head. Corruption had wormed its way into high places. The Secretary of Interior and other important officials were later found guilty in the greatest official exposure of governmental corruption since Grant's administration. The Democrats might have made political capital out of these prosecutions, but they were suffering from internal dissension. The liberal Republicans, headed by LaFollette and Norris, won most of the laurels for exposing the administration.

Despite the temporary embarrassment, the Republicans had little difficulty in retaining their dominant position. Coolidge was to be the candidate, and no one could imagine any connection between him and corruption. Few men in American public life ever surpassed Calvin Coolidge in public esteem. Citizens of all classes accepted unquestioningly his claim to honesty and integrity, though many disagreed with his political views. The divided Democratic party held its now famous 1924 convention in New York. For more than one hundred ballots (a record for political inanity), the forces of William G. McAdoo, the dry, battled those of Governor Alfred E. Smith, the wet. After all chance of unifying the party had been destroyed, the empty honor went to John W. Davis, a leading conservative lawyer.

The selection of Coolidge and Davis did little to allay a growing unrest in the agricultural sections. Emerging from the war period, with its high prices and its optimistic psychology, American farmers found themselves, by 1922, in the worst predicament of a century. With farms geared to the high production level of the war years, when American farmers were feeding America and the Allied armies, the rapid drop in prices for farm products threatened agriculture with bankruptcy. Prices were in many cases below the cost of production, even if the farmer did not value his own labor at anything. Taxes and interest charges, based upon the agricultural prosperity of the war years, were too often greater than the entire money value of a farm's produce. The depression of the early twenties was more telling than that of Cleveland's second administration, because agriculture had not been on an industrial basis in 1893. In the intervening thirty years, farming had ceased to be a way of life and had become an industrial enterprise. The new status placed farmers in greater danger of foreclosure and the incidental loss of all equities in the land.

When neither of the major parties did more than insert pious resolutions in its party platform, the agricultural leaders prevailed upon the veteran Robert M. LaFollette to launch a new Progressive party. Labor leaders joined in the movement, and Senator Burton K. Wheeler, of Montana, was selected as the vice-presidential candidate. Though handicapped by lack of funds and local organization, the LaFollette Progressives polled almost five million votes, to eight million for Davis, and fifteen million for Coolidge. In eleven states La Follette out-polled the Democratic ticket, and in seven others there was practically an even division of the opposition strength between them. Thus, despite a two-and-one-half-million-vote increase over 1920, the Democrats lost almost a million, and the Republicans almost half a million votes. It was the worst Democratic defeat since 1860.

The Coolidge administration refused to take cognizance of economic storm warnings. The United States was moving ever closer to an economic crisis. Business booster clubs emphasized confidence and service. Calvin Coolidge urged citizens not "to sell America short." The farmer's plight was not improved; he was only becoming inured to it. In order to dispose of their products, manufacturers were relying upon the future earning power of consumers; thus, installment buying became a prominent part of distribution economics. Large amounts of American money had found investment opportunities abroad, and when those opportunities became fewer, increasing sums were thrown upon the stock market. Stock prices went higher and returns relatively lower.

It was in this uncertain economic half-light that Herbert Hoover was nominated by the Republicans. Citizens felt an unexpressed fear that all was not well, but Hoover had earned a reputation as a "social engineer." He could plan for the nation! That, after all, was the real job of the President. With his slide-rule, his logarithms, and his uncanny business judgment (a sort of sixth sense), he would straighten out the little inconsistencies in the economic order.

LaFollette had died in June, 1925, and with him went the possibility of continuing the Progressive experiment. The Democrats were therefore in a better position to increase their membership, even though few leaders had illusions of national victory. The breach of 1924 had to be closed and, with a rising tide of opinion against prohibition in the populous centers, the breach could not be closed by nominating a prohibitionist. The party must move into the industrial states if it hoped to become a threat to Republican hegemony. Governor Alfred E. Smith, of New York, was therefore the unanimous choice of the party leaders. The dry Democrats had to swallow a bitter dose, more bitter because of their 1924 convention experience. The 1928 convention, held in Houston, Texas, was a triumph for him who had launched his career in an East Side fish market. The new urban civilization was building its precedents, its catch-words, and its political clichés. Urban dwellers had difficulty in generating emotion for log-cabins, rail-splitting, meager school facilities, and other such catch phrases of ruraldom. But "Al" Smith was likened to Lincoln, as one who epitomized the existence of opportunity in the United States, as one who had come from lowly beginnings to the highest honor that may be conferred by a major political party—representing the will of millions of American citizens.

The Republican publicity corps was not ineffective. Hoover had been born in a log cabin, and, from the privations of his early years in Iowa, had developed those virtues of agrarian democracy—honesty, frugality, and Christian sacrifice—which had followed him throughout his colorful career as an engineer, philanthropist, director of relief to the stricken people of war-torn Europe, and government official. Like Rousseau's natural man, Hoover had an almost unlimited capacity for pity. From 1918 to 1928, he was loved by the American people as the country's greatest humanitarian.

For the first time since 1916, the issues between the parties were reasonably sharp. It was Republican against Democrat, Protestant against Catholic, property against human rights, prohibitionist against anti-prohibitionist, and ruralism against urbanism. Of course, the American people could not

THE BATTLE FOR BALLOTS

be divided into two crisply defined groups, in which the Republicans unequivocally supported Protestantism, order, *laissez faire*, and the rural virtues, while the Democrats opposed all of them. Party affiliation represents more mental travail than such a simple formula would imply.

In the election, the humanitarian and social engineer swamped the representative of the new urbanism, the Republican percentage being surpassed only by the 1920 mark. But Smith increased the 1924 Democratic total by 71.4 per cent. More than that, he had breathed into the party the will to win. The defeatism that has characterized Democratic leadership from 1919 to 1928 gave way to a new spirit, a militancy not present since Wilson, who, with brief case full of notes, had conducted seminars for members of Congress.

Herbert Hoover had scarcely settled himself in the presidential chair when "Black Friday" destroyed any possibility for a successful administration. As a back drop to Coolidge's "I do not choose to run," in 1928, Grace Coolidge is said to have remarked, "Poppa says there's a depression coming." And come it did on that memorable October day in 1929. The bottom dropped out of everything, and especially out of the spirit of the enigmatic decade which followed the war. The optimism of 1928 went out of thirty-story windows in the pockets of speculators caught short in the market. Bankers who had earnestly, and perhaps honestly, sought to put the depositors' money to work for hire, had no alternative to closing their banks when the depositors called for their savings. Factories were closed, and crops were not worth the cost of harvesting. Armies of unemployed walked the streets in search of jobs they knew did not exist. To put it simply, America was stunned; the "chosen people" accolade which Americans had bestowed upon themselves was cast aside as a contagion. Leaders began to speak the truth—America was paying the price imposed by a fifteen-year vacation from the responsibility of thinking out its economic and social problems. The whole catastrophe might have been averted if people had been less willing to die for, and more willing to think for, their country

The Hoover administration stumbled through the remaining three years, years that were characterized by a vaulting demand for business reform. People forgot that they had supported the business program in increasing numbers during the preceding three elections. Though the darlings of the Artificial Decade, the corporation leaders were anathematized as responsible, through their selfishness, for the debacle.

Running for re-election, President Hoover blamed the world depression for the temporary dislocation of the economic machine. But for that there might have been "two chickens in every pot and two cars in every garage." He even went so far as to prophesy that grass would grow in the streets of our great cities if the voters listened to the call of the siren and installed a Democratic administration in Washington. "The Democrats were notoriously inefficient in directing an economic order." Cleveland had met with ruin in 1893, and only the war saved Woodrow Wilson!

From a veritable crowd of aspiring candidates, the Chicago Democratic convention selected Franklin Delano Roosevelt, governor of New York, as its candidate, with the veteran house member from Texas, John Nance Garner, as his running-mate. On account of his incalculable contribution to the party *esprit de corps*, there was considerable support for the nomination of Smith again. But, with roseate hopes for victory, the party leaders, shunning certain internecine strife, agreed upon the more politic choice. Gratitude for Smith's services was paid by resolution rather than by nomination.

The demand for governmental intervention welled up from the entire country. The opposite policy had resulted in the loss of jobs and of property. Not since 1914 had the country been so conscious of economic reform. Roosevelt's promise to protect the interests of the common citizen was enough to change the party affiliation of five million Hoover supporters of 1928. The Democratic canvass was increased almost eight millions over the surprising Smith total of 1928, and fourteen and one-half millions over the 1924 vote. On the other hand, Hoover's vote dropped from 21,392,196 to 15,161,841, in spite of a three-million increase in the electorate.

The 1932 election represented a major realignment of party membership. Only 1856 and 1896 can be regarded as approximating it in intensity, but the numbers involved in 1932 were far greater. The new administration took its mandate for intervention seriously, equaling, if not surpassing, the record of Woodrow Wilson's first two years in the White House. The country approved. More fortunate than Wilson's administration, Roosevelt's government was not dissuaded by outside factors from the task of finding solutions. And in 1936, Roosevelt was re-elected over his Republican opponent, Governor Alfred M. Landon, of Kansas, by an increased margin. Roosevelt's share of the forty-five million popular votes (60 per cent) was less than one-half of one per cent under the highest mark set by President Harding in 1920. Only two states—Maine and Vermont—

cast their electoral votes for the Republican nominee. This election was the greatest victory of the Democrats since the Civil War and the worst of the Republicans' seven national defeats.

Summary

The story of the last nineteen national elections is an interpretation of American political theory. When the Civil War and its aftermath were out of the way, the great political issues revolved about the question of how far the government should go in bringing the good life to the common man. The rise of the industrial order brought this dominant problem into the area of political discussion. The history of American legislation since 1880 is one of increasing governmental regulation of business on one side and of increasing concentration of economic power upon the other.

The advocates of an unrestrained economic order pleaded to the Constitution and to the marvelous advance of economic enterprise in America. No one will deny either that the "fathers" believed in a high degree of *laissez faire* or that this country's industrial order is the most efficient in the world. But, relative to the first contention, it must be understood that the fathers of the Constitution were fearful of governmental tyranny. This fear was omnipresent in the political atmosphere in the last half of the eighteenth century. The doctrine of natural rights increased in importance; the Constitution must be regarded as a document of that fear and of that philosophy. On the other hand, the fathers could scarcely have been expected to anticipate the problems that would arise under an industrial order. It must be remembered that theirs was an agrarian perspective. Their fear

THE BATTLE FOR BALLOTS

was of government monopolies. To take from government the right to create monopolies was their solution. No one can reasonably contend that they had no objection to monopolies that were not governmental creations.

In *Figure 2*, the party percentages of the last twenty elections are shown. The behavior of the graph lines offers suffi-

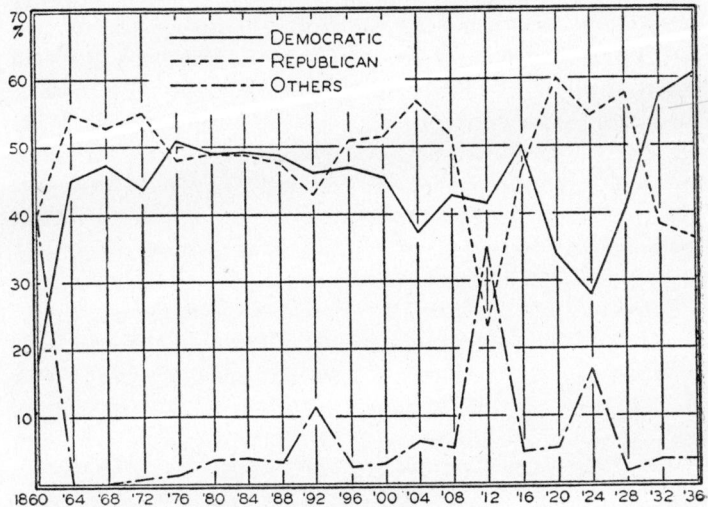

Figure 2.—Percentage Popular Votes: by Parties

cient logic for the four-period division. The War and Reconstruction era shows the Republicans falling from their dominant position of over 50 per cent in the first three elections (1864, 1868, 1872) to one below the Democrats in 1876. Then comes the second period, marked by its remarkable consistency. In none of the four elections did a party receive a majority of the popular vote, and in only one did either of the major parties drop below the 45 per cent mark.[7] The period is characterized, however, by the rise along the base line of the strength of those voters who favored governmental intervention.

The third period is one of different complexion. The union with the Populists made the Democrats into a party pledged to business regulation. And though the Republicans outstripped them in the early part of the period, their strength rose steadily from 1904 to 1916. The final period is difficult; the graph lines behave in senseless fashion. The old party loyalty of the period from 1864 to 1896 is gone. In the five elections the Democrats present a divergence of thirty-one percentage points, the Republicans one of twenty-four. Contrast this record with that of the second period when the Republicans, the variable party, had a divergence of only 5.4 percentage points between the high of 1880 and their low of 1892. Therein lies all the evidence that is necessary to prove that something happened in American politics after 1892.

If the European war had not occurred to divert the attention of people from the question of governmental intervention, the Republican split (of 1912) might have produced a realignment of voters into a party system in which, for a time, one party would have definitely opposed interventionism and the other supported it. Thereafter, the programs would probably have been formulated upon the bases of relatively more and relatively less governmental interference. Thus, today (1940) the issues which lie before the American people are those which they might, in principle, have faced in 1916.

---

[7] The Republican mark in 1892 was slightly under 43 per cent.

★ ★ ★ ★ ★

CHAPTER TWO

Sectionalism Preferred

★ ★ ★ ★ ★ ★ ★ ★

THE nine states of the East, comprising New England and the three upper North Atlantic states (New York, New Jersey, and Pennsylvania) have stood continuously since the Civil War above each of the other four sections in population, and have been exceeded only by the Middle West in the number of ballots cast for presidential electors. The average population percentages, in relation to the other sections, were 31.8 per cent, 28.8 per cent, 28.3 per cent, and 28.1 per cent for the four periods. This means that, since 1880, the section has grown in population at about the same ratio as the remainder of the country, in spite of the industrial development of the Middle West and the phenomenal population increases of the Southwest and of the Pacific littoral.

The Republican dominance of the East derived essentially in economic factors. As the leading manufacturing and commercial section, its interests were materially improved through the instrumentality of a protective tariff. Since the twenties of last century, the East has labored incessantly for tariff increases. Daniel Webster did valiant service in the adoption of Henry Clay's formula for national prosperity. This insistence upon economic advantage for industry bred its own antithesis. The sections producing raw materials—such as the South with its rice, cotton, and tobacco; and the Middle West with its wheat, corn, and meat—became extremely conscious of their "colonial" status. They were being exploited, economically and politically, by a favored section. If the South had not insisted upon the retention of slavery in contradiction to the emergent demand of agrarian democracy for equality and freedom, the "colonial" sections might well have retained the control of national politics which they established under Andrew Jackson, at least until, seeking economic salvation, they had fostered their own infant industries and thereby had succeeded in dissipating the industrial concentration of the East. In the language of Scott Nearing, this would have constituted a "revolt of the nuclei."

The struggle over slavery intervened to prevent the consummation of this natural solution, and in the organization of the new Republican party, the East, being preponderantly influential in that movement, protected its economic interests. In the platform of 1856 no mention was made of tariff, but in that of 1860 there was included a strong plank for protection. From that time, the party has unwaveringly supported the protection principle. In 1860 the Middle West might well have opposed the tariff but for its adherence to the Union, freedom, and democracy. The Republican party was, therefore, at its inception, a combination of idealism concerning human rights and of practical politics concerning favoritism to industry.

The Civil War made the East and Middle West joint partners in the defense of the Constitution, the flag, and the Union. The two sections were bound together, for better or for worse, pending the emergence of a new generation of

SECTIONALISM PREFERRED

voters whose motivating personal experiences were had in peaceful pursuits rather than on battlefields in another section of the country. As the industrial order grew from the stripling that it had been in 1860, its leaders found their places in the Republican party. And before the Middle West was released from the grip of the war memories, the new industrialism had expanded into Ohio, Indiana, Michigan, and Illinois. Thus, the section came to have a definite interest in the retention of the tariff as an instrument of national policy. The East's interests were, meanwhile, being served by the Republican party.

Despite the strong influence of industrialism, the East displayed continuous anti-tariff strength. Commerce, in the sense of navigation, flourishes under a system of unrestricted trade. More ships would be employed if there were more imports, and increasing import volume could be balanced financially only by large export trade. Thus the commercial interests of the three states lying proximate to the trade bottle-neck of the New York port (Connecticut, New York, and New Jersey) were sufficiently strong to challenge the East's point of view on tariff. From 1864 to 1892, inclusive, the low-tariff Democrats out-polled the Republicans in these three states, 49.23 per cent to 49.06 per cent. These figures are in decided contrast to the ratios in the six eastern states more interested in manufacturing and agriculture, where the Democrats received but 42.19 per cent to 55.69 per cent for the Republicans.

As a whole, however, the East was preponderantly a Republican section throughout the period. In only four of the nineteen elections did that party fail to secure an absolute majority of popular votes. From 1864 to 1936, the East cast

PRESIDENTIAL ELECTIONS

an accumulative total of more than one hundred and two million votes for presidential electors, 52.2 per cent of which went to the Republicans, 42.8 per cent to the Democrats, and over 5 per cent to minor parties.[1] The Republican percentages of the five sections for each of the nineteen elections are shown in *Figure 3*. Only in 1892, 1912, 1932, and 1936 did the party

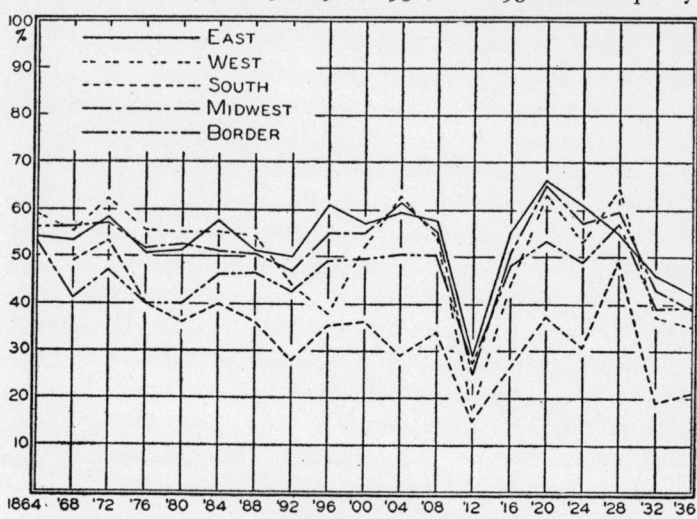

Figure 3.—Sectional Percentages of Republican Vote

[1] The following figures show the vote totals for the East, 1864-1936.

Party	1864-1876	1880-1892	1896-1916	1920-1936	1864-1936
Republicans	4,824,639	6,581,865	13,227,138	28,832,981	53,466,623
Democrats	4,075,138	5,913,753	9,740,439	24,141,406	43,870,736
Others	28,926	388,676	2,119,090	2,600,585	5,137,277
Total	8,917,003	12,884,294	25,166,667	55,574,972	102,542,936

SECTIONALISM PREFERRED

of Lincoln, Blaine, and Theodore Roosevelt fail to command a popular majority. And only in the latter two years did the Democrats replace the Republicans as the majority party. In 1892, Harrison carried the section over Cleveland, but minor parties polled enough votes to reduce the Republican poll to 49.2 per cent. In 1912, William Howard Taft's vote was but 27.4 per cent of the section's total. Yet the East led all other sections in supporting the conservative Republican ticket in that election. The 1912 Democratic mark was but 38.1 per cent which, incidentally, was identical with the Bryan percentage of 1908. This indicates that the Republican split of 1912 did not result in any relative increase in the Democratic vote, a fact which is quite contrary to the observations of some analysts. Even though Wilson was a candidate from the section, he polled approximately twenty-seven thousand fewer eastern votes than Bryan had in 1908.

With its threat of governmental intervention, the election of 1896 was instrumental in increasing the dominance of the Republicans in the East. Except for the maverick election of 1912, this dominance lasted for more than thirty years. The fusionist program was essentially an agrarian reaction against industrial and financial monopoly, against the grip that bankers were securing upon the industrial machine. Bryan and his cohorts felt what Veblen graphically described in his *Engineers and the Price System*. But eastern agriculture, which fifty years before might have sympathized with an agrarian program, shrank from what it regarded as the radicalism of the Populist program. The farm problems of the East were not those of the great hinterland. Though the entire agricultural industry may have been receiving less than justice in the American national economy, the farmers of the

East were favorably situated with regard to the great urban markets; they were not the unwitting victims of high freight rates; and they had already achieved a decided diversification in agricultural production that released them from complete dependence upon the world price of some staple product like wheat or cotton.

Workmen with jobs in the industrial regiment, and the merchants and farmers, who depended upon the consuming

TABLE I.—EFFECT OF 1896 ELECTION ON PARTY ALLEGIANCE IN THE EAST

	1892		1896		1908	
	Republican	Democrat	Republican	Democrat	Republican	Democrat
Maine	62,878	48,024	80,461	34,587	66,987	35,403
N. H.	45,658	42,081	57,444	21,650	53,149	33,655
Vt.	37,992	16,325	50,991	10,607	39,552	11,496
Mass.	202,927	176,858	278,976	121,385	265,966	155,543
R. I.	26,975	24,336	37,437	14,459	43,942	24,706
Conn.	77,032	82,395	110,285	56,740	112,915	68,255
N. Y.	609,459	654,900	819,838	551,513	870,070	667,468
N. J.	156,101	171,066	221,371	133,695	265,326	182,567
Penn.	516,011	452,264	728,300	433,228	745,779	448,782
Total	1,735,033	1,668,249	2,385,103	1,377,864	2,463,686	1,628,875

power of workers, were afraid of the consequences of a Democratic triumph. The price of individual freedom might be too great! Republican propagandists kept the wraith of economic debacle constantly before the people of the section. The result was the highest Republican percentage of the section's popular vote from 1856 to 1916. The measure of this stampede to the business party, by states, is depicted in TABLE I.

SECTIONALISM PREFERRED

The importance of the 1896 scare-campaign lay not so much in the swollen Republican totals as in the fact that the change of allegiance was permanent. In each of the nine states, Bryan's vote was less than that of Cleveland in 1892. *Figure 4* gives the Democratic percentages for each section in each election. In New Hampshire the Democratic loss

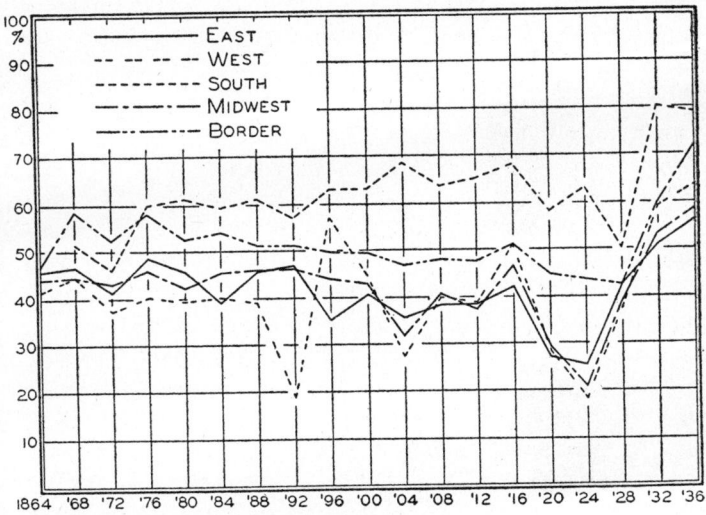

Figure 4.—Sectional Percentages of Democratic Vote

was 48.6 per cent; in Rhode Island, 40.6 per cent; and in Pennsylvania, the least of the nine, 4.2 per cent. Not only did the Democrats lose 17.4 per cent of the 1892 vote, but the Republicans secured a 37.5 per cent accretion. In Connecticut their gain was 43.2 per cent; in New Jersey, 41.8 per cent; in Pennsylvania, 41.1 per cent; in Massachusetts,

37.4 per cent, and in New York, 34.8 per cent. New Hampshire brought up the rear with only 25.8 per cent. Not all of this increase, however, came from Democratic ranks; most of it came from those habitual non-voters who exercise their franchise privilege only when danger threatens. In 1892, the adult-participation ratio per thousand had dropped off from 352.4 to 338.9. It rose in 1896 to 351.3. In 1892 the issues were not clear-cut; there were three candidates in the race. When more than two major candidates seek the presidential office, voters seem to become confused and large numbers refrain from voting.[2]

The Republicans maintained their high percentage marks through 1900, 1904, and, as is seen in both the graph (*Figure 3*) and the table (1), through 1908. There was, however, a slight easing off in 1900, as the habitual non-voters, having saved the country four years before, drifted back into the ranks of the political onlookers. Not one state wavered from the ranks of the "solid" East from 1896 to 1908. Thirty-six contests without a single apostasy! In 1912, Vermont went for Taft, Pennsylvania for Roosevelt, and the other seven for Wilson upon a minority basis. Except for New Hampshire, they were all back behind Hughes in 1916, but with slighter majorities than before the schism of 1912.

The Artificial Decade was inaugurated with the highest popular percentages of the nineteen elections. The 1920 Republican percentage for the East was 66.3 per cent; the Democrats dropped off to 27.3 per cent. Vermont gave

[2] In 1892, the adult-participation ratio fell off 13.3 percentage points and in 1912, 15.9 points. In 1924, with women not yet habituated to voting, the ratio increased 2.6 points, but in the next election (1928) it skyrocketed 75.9 points. The latter, like 1896, presented a reasonably simple problem in voter conviction with only Hoover and Smith seriously in the race.

Harding and Coolidge 75.9 per cent of its vote. In 1924 the marks of both parties declined to 60.9 per cent and 25.8 per cent, respectively, because of the support which organized labor gave to LaFollette. The first break from the monotonous regularity of Republican successes after 1916 came in 1928. Both Massachusetts and Rhode Island gave Governor Smith slight majorities. In 1932, New York and New

TABLE 2.—RISE OF DEMOCRATIC STRENGTH IN THE EAST, 1920-1936

	1920	1924	1928	1932	1936
Me.	58,961	41,964	81,179	128,907	126,333
N. H.	62,662	57,201	80,715	100,680	108,460
Vt.	20,919	16,124	44,440	56,266	62,144
Mass.	276,691	280,884	792,758	800,148	942,716
R. I.	55,062	76,606	118,973	146,604	164,541
Conn.	120,721	110,184	252,040	281,632	382,129
N. Y.	731,238	950,796	2,089,863	2,534,959	3,293,222
N. J.	258,229	298,043	616,517	806,630	1,083,549
Penn.	503,202	409,192	1,067,586	1,295,948	2,353,788
Total East	2,087,685	2,240,994	5,144,071	6,151,774	8,516,882

Jersey joined these innovators, and in 1936 only Maine and Vermont remained to wave triumphantly the flag of Republicanism.[3] Yet in both 1932 and 1936, the East led all sections in support of the "Grand Old Party."

From its nadir of 1924, the Democratic party's record is one of phenomenal increase in eastern popularity. The section's Democratic marks for those four elections were

[3] The Republican losses, in percentage points, from 1920 to 1936 were as follows: Maine, 11.8; New Hampshire, 11.8; Vermont, 19.5; Massachusetts, 26.8; Rhode Island, 23.9; Connecticut, 20.7; New York, 26.8; New Jersey, 28.1; and Pennsylvania, 24.9; New Jersey's drop was from 67.7 per cent to 39.6 per cent.

25.8 per cent, 42.7 per cent, 50.3 per cent, and 56.7 per cent. The arithmetical story of this rise of fortune is shown in TABLE 2.

The statistics reveal the amazing rise of Democratic prestige in the East. Though five states showed decreased Democratic polls in 1924, of the remaining twenty-seven opportunities for increase or decrease only Maine in 1936 showed a decrease. The 1928 Massachusetts accretion over the preceding election's Democratic total was 182.2 per cent. Massachusetts had supported Governor Smith in the New York convention. Its citizens showed little enthusiasm for John W. Davis. But when Smith received the 1928 nomination, the Democratic vote leaped from 280,884 to 792,758. On the other hand, Republican 1932 and 1936 totals were in each case under those of 1928. However, in 1936, the Republican vote in Maine, Hew Hampshire, Vermont, Massachusetts, Rhode Island, New York, and Pennsylvania increased over that of 1932, but none of these gains could be viewed as sensational.

A brief summary of the state aspects of these nineteen presidential elections may prove helpful. For this purpose, the six New England states may be considered to have had, in these nineteen elections, a total of 114 separate contests.[4] Of these, the Republicans won all but eighteen, or 84.2 per cent. Moreover, five of these losses occurred in 1912, the year of the Great Schism. And eight came from 1928 to

[4] A presidential election is not one great contest in the United States. Rather, it is forty-eight separate and individual elections. Unfortunately, there exists no accepted uncomplicated terminology for these "elections in states." They are not to be misinterpreted as state elections, or elections for the selection of state officers, even though a state election and a national election in a state may simultaneously occur. Except for Maine, the distinction is sheerly functional rather than temporal.

1936! Thus, of the other eighty-four contests, the Republicans took all but five, for a record of 94 per cent. This country may be witnessing the beginning of a new order in New England, but prophecies in the teeth of tradition are hazardous. Vermont holds the distinction of having given its electoral vote to the Republicans in each of the nineteen elections. It is the only state with such a record of Republican consistency. With Utah, it supported Taft in 1912, and with Maine it voted for Landon in 1936. When some partisan Republican is deploring the slavishness of Georgia voters, the record of Vermont should be called to his attention.

Maine has an untarnished Republican record, with one exception—1912—and even then it barely went to Wilson over the Progressive ticket. New Hampshire has thrice filled the apostate's rôle,[5] Massachusetts and Rhode Island, four times;[6] while Connecticut has been the black sheep of Yankeedom with six Democratic triumphs.[7]

Of the other three states of the East, Pennsylvania has earned the title of "Republican Commonwealth." Not until 1936 did it give its vote to a Democrat, even though it followed the first Roosevelt in 1912. New York has supported the Republicans twelve, and the Democrats seven, times;[8] while New Jersey has gone Democratic ten times to nine for

---

[5] 1912, 1916, and 1936.

[6] Curiously enough, they broke across in the same elections—1912, 1928, 1932, and 1936.

[7] 1876, 1884, 1888, 1892, 1912, and 1936.

[8] 1868, 1876, 1884, 1892, 1912, 1932, and 1936. Incidentally, in omly one of these elections did New York cast its ballot for other than a former governor of the state who was a candidate for the presidency. Those former governors were Seymour (1868), Tilden (1876), Cleveland (1884 and 1892), and Franklin D. Roosevelt (1932 and 1936). Woodrow Wilson, of neighboring New Jersey, was the only candidate not a former governor of the state who won the state for the Democrats, and he received less than 42 per cent of the vote.

the Republicans.[9] In the fifty-seven contests in these three states, the Republicans won thirty-eight, or 66.6 per cent. Thus, in the 171 contests in the nine eastern states, the Republicans have won 134, or 78.4 per cent.

The Border Marches

The American Border Marches, stretching from Delaware Bay to the mouth of the Kaw, stand politically as the most unperturbed of the five geographic sections. The five states —Delaware, Maryland, West Virginia, Kentucky, and Missouri—represent a diversity of economic enterprise. By and large, agriculture is the basic industry, but the coal fields of West Virginia, the manufacturing activities of Delaware and Missouri, and the commercial interests of Maryland contribute to that leavening which comes with diversification. None of the five relies for its prosperity upon a single staple product, industrial or agricultural. This balance in economy has produced a political stability, but not a stagnation. For in the past eighty years, pronounced general trends have operated in these Border states.

In the first place, all five were slave states before the Civil War, but in each of them there were large numbers of small holdings. The plantation system, except in parts of Maryland and Delaware, was not practicable. The part taken by the upper states in the slave-holding economy was that of breeding slaves for the market, a rather profitable business

[9] 1864, 1868, 1876, 1880, 1884, 1888, 1892, 1912, 1932, and 1936. Thus from 1864 to 1892, the Republicans won but one election (1872); but from 1896 to 1928, the Democrats won only the election of 1912, when Wilson barely defeated Theodore Roosevelt. In that election the Democrats were a plurality choice, receiving but 40.5 per cent of the total popular vote.

SECTIONALISM PREFERRED

after the ban was clamped upon the importation of slaves from the West Indies. The interests of the Border in the slavery question were therefore of secondary character; no fundamental economy was threatened. The leaders of the Border reacted to the Civil War much the same as politicians generally react to political questions like the tariff, or wages and hours legislation. And, in 1861, those economic interests were not sufficiently compelling to take the Border states into the Confederacy.

Despite their refusal to cast their lot with "Secessia," the five states were, in 1860, predominantly Democratic.[10] The Republican vote was a mere trickle, amounting to but 5.8 per cent of the total. Over 40 per cent went to Bell, of the Constitutional Union party, who ran upon a platform of compromise for the sake of preserving the Union. Douglas, the northern Democrat, received 21.7 per cent, and Breckenridge, the southern Democrat, 31.9 per cent. Thus, over 68 per cent of that critical vote was against the die-hard attitude of the southern slavocracy.

The Democractic complexion of the Border states per-

[10] The votes of the four Border States in 1860 (West Virginia was not yet a state) were:

State	Lincoln Republican	Douglas Northern Democrat	Breckenridge Southern Democrat	Bell Const.Union	Total
Delaware	3,815	1,023	7,337	3,864	16,039
Kentucky	1,364	25,651	53,143	66,058	146,216
Maryland	2,294	5,966	42,482	41,760	92,502
Missouri	17,028	58,801	31,317	58,372	165,718
Total Border	24,501	91,441	134,279	170,054	420,475

sisted even in the war election of 1864, for, though going safely for the Lincoln-Johnson Union ticket, General McClellan received 46.2 per cent of the popular vote. The Border led all other sections in support of the Democratic ticket. In 1868 and 1872, it was again the Democratic vanguard. In 1876, the South's rejuvenated Democracy crowded the Border from leadership. In this first period, there were strong reasons for the Border's high Democratic percentages.[11] Whole classes were not disfranchised, as in the South, for their participation in the rebellion. The states of the Border had smaller percentages of slaves, in relation to the whole population; the emergence of Negro suffrage, therefore, did not wrest control from the dominant white party. As many of the important military campaigns were fought in Border states, there was increasing opposition to the war and to the Republicans who were, in the eyes of Border victims, responsible for it. The Border suffered more than any other section in the earlier years of the conflict. The hatreds and emotions generated then were slow in disappearing from the scene of Border politics.

After 1876, the Democratic party of the Border States was victim of slow decline, which, on account of its persistence,

[11] The Border votes in the four periods were as follows:

	Republican	Democratic	Others	Total
1864-1876	1,050,044	1,305,453	14,701	2,370,288
1880-1892	2,016,710	2,400,639	187,518	4,604,867
1896-1916	4,539,787	4,923,728	598,037	10,061,552
1920-1936	8,650,664	9,421,248	365,665	18,437,577
Total 1864-1936	16,257,205	18,051,068	1,165,921	35,474,284

approximated the serenity of cosmic decision. After each of the six elections immediately succeeding that of 1876, the Border politicians must have realized that the Republican tortoise was steadily reducing the lead which the Democratic hare had established in the Reconstruction contests. In 1892, the tortoise was still some distance back; in 1896, his breath was upon the heels of the straining hare; in 1900, he ran nose to shoulder; and in 1904, the tenacious tortoise was out in front. Until 1932, he stayed there except for 1912 and 1916. In the last two races (1932 and 1936) an unconscionable weight handicap made the tortoise's efforts practically hopeless from the start.

Being the minority party in the early period, the Republicans effected their rise to power by fits and starts. The graph line in *Figure 3* shows this irregularity. When third parties made their appearances, the Republican vote totals fell in proportion to the strength commanded by the interlopers. For minor parties gather the malcontents and enemies of the ruling parties. When those elements are united in a single party, its vote naturally increases. For instance, in 1888, the Republicans polled 582,516 votes in the five Border states. In 1892, that figure was reduced by almost thirty thousand. The Populists had challenged the Republicans' opposition rôle. But, in 1896, with no effective minor-party opposition, the Republican vote vaulted to 719,744, an increase over 1892 of 29.5 per cent. The Democratic increase for the same election was but 17.2 per cent.

Though fusion with the Populists materially improved the Democratic strength in some sections, such was not the case in the Border. The Democratic popular vote percentage dropped from 51 per cent to 50 per cent in 1896, while that of the Republicans rose from 42.7 per cent to 48.2 per cent. Fusion was popular in Missouri and to some extent in Kentucky, but it was resented in Delaware and Maryland, where the party's 1896 vote declined 27.1 per cent and 8 per cent, respectively. These two states reflected the East's skepticism of the Bryan program. Their agricultural situation was not so critical as, for example, that of Missouri. Moreover, business was invading the eastern Border states, and large numbers of industrial and commercial workers feared an even worse economic depression than that under Cleveland.

There is still another factor in the coldness with which the Border viewed the interventionist Bryanism. In the upland sections of Maryland, West Virginia, Kentucky, and southern Missouri were millions of people who were still thinking and acting in conformity to the principles of agrarian democracy and its individualistic philosophy. These were not "hillbillies" in any derogatory sense; they were simply people to whom tradition was the motivating factor in their political behavior. Removed from the crossroads of the country's march to the new industrial civilization, they were not cognizant of the great problems following in the wake of industrial expansion. Credit, market, and the good life were generally community rather than sectional or national problems. Any suggestion, therefore, dealing with the freedom of individual initiative was viewed as an unnecessary evil and one that should not for one moment be tolerated.

Accounts of monopoly exploitation, of unconscionable labor practices, and of denials of civil rights, that found their way back to these hillside farms and villages had little more meaning than the stories of abuses abroad. Justice was still an individual or, at best, a community concept. If a moun-

SECTIONALISM PREFERRED

taineer thought that his employer was treating him unfairly, the controversy concerned only himself and his employer. If pacific methods were abortive, there was always the trusty rifle above the door. The condition of this people's isolation had preserved in them a firm conviction in the accepted principles of freedom and equality, and they were as skeptical as peasants of innovation.

This spirit of individual integrity, achieved without the trappings of regulatory laws and snooping inspectors, flared extravagantly in the election of 1896. In Kentucky, opposition to governmental interference had for decades been measured by the people's supreme hatred of United States revenue officers. The hillman's enmity was distinctly personal. It mattered little that the officer might be legally performing the duties of his office—he ought to have had more manliness than to accept such responsibilities! In Kentucky, the 1896 Republican poll was 61 per cent greater than that of 1892.[12] In Maryland and West Virginia, the increase was 47.7 per cent and 31.2 per cent, respectively.[13]

The election of 1892 terminated a thirty-two year period of Democratic dominance in the Border states. In those eight elections, the Democrats amassed 53.1 per cent of the total votes to 44 per cent for the Republicans. In the next nine elections (1896-1928), the latter received 49.4 per cent to the Democrats' 46.2 per cent. However, the Border gave 60.3 per cent of its vote to Franklin D. Roosevelt in the last

[12] The Republicans carried Kentucky for the first time, the vote being 218,171 to 217,890 for the Democrats, with minor parties polling 9,895 votes.

[13] The Democrats lost 8 per cent in Maryland and gained 24.2 per cent in Kentucky, and 11.8 per cent in West Virginia.

two elections, while the Republican share dropped to 38.8 per cent, lowest in the entire period.[14]

Before 1896, the Democrats took thirty-three of the forty individual contests, all seven of the Republican victories coming during Reconstruction and before 1876. From 1876 to 1892, the Democrats swept the twenty-five contests without a loss. However, from 1896 to 1928, the Republicans took twenty-seven of the forty-five contests and split with the Democrats in four others. When the ten contests of 1932 and 1936 are included, the Democratic total was twenty-four out of fifty-five, to twenty-seven for the Republicans.[15]

West Virginia, with eleven triumphs in the nineteen elections, and Delaware with ten, led the section for the Republicans. Kentucky was the most Democratic, with only three Republican triumphs. Missouri had four, and Maryland six, victories for that party.[16]

The South

From the point of view of partisan politics, the South is the most consistent of the five sections. Its strong Democratic preference originated in the two decades before 1860, but it has persisted with monotonous regularity since 1876. In many ways, the South is an enigma. Priding itself in Jeffersonianism, it denied many of the fundamental principles of that American physiocracy. The southern Jeffersonians in

[14] The marks for the entire period (1864-1936) were Republican 46.3 per cent Democratic 50.3 per cent, and others 3.3 per cent.

[15] The split slectoral votes were Kentucky (1896), Maryland (1904 and 1908), and West Virginia (1916).

[16] The split decisions of Kentucky, Maryland, and West Virginia were allocated to the party receiving a majority of the state's electoral-college delegation. If popular-vote plurality were the criterion, two Maryland elections recorded, for the Democrats would have to be placed in the category of Republican triumph.

SECTIONALISM PREFERRED

the era before Jackson were to be found in the piedmont and hill sections, where land ownership and free enterprise formed a natural basis for democracy. The great plantation owners, prototypes of modern agricultural industrialists, stood against the interests of these equalitarians of the back country. Slavery and small-holdings economies were antithetical especially after cotton became the profitable staple product of the section. Competition between the systems was only less spectacular than that between the rancher and the dirt-farmer on the fringes of the "Great American Desert" in the eighties of last century.

With its labor supply at hand, the plantation system moved farther back into the hills, as well as expanding westward into the virgin domain of Texas. In either case, it came in contact with the small holder. The Jeffersonians followed the leadership of the dynamic Jackson, and more and more, the plantation owners found themselves in the coalition against the agrarian democrats. The importance of the southern Whig leaders in national politics from 1835 to 1850 has been underestimated. With the assistance of those who feared violence, the southern Whigs secured the enactment of the fugitive slave law. But after the northern agrarians, philosophic executors of the Jeffersonian doctrine, formed the Republican party as a method of forcing their ideas of equality and free enterprise upon the whole country, former Whig leaders became the backbone of the sectional coalition.

In the *ante bellum* period, the South was more influential in national politics than any other section. In the presidential office, in the Cabinet, and on the Supreme Court, it found the means of protecting itself from superior human fecundity and from the more dynamic political philosophy of the East and Middle West. Even as early as 1820, the date of the Missouri Compromise, the South was fighting a rear-guard action. From thence until the war, it retained its parity by political mechanics, by bluff, and by appeal to the Constitution. Losing relatively in congressional representation, the section clung to the Supreme Court as the last line of defense. And when that body made its unfortunate decision in the Dred Scott case, the crisis was at hand. Either the South had to back down politically and accept the inevitable consequences of that action which included the forthright abolition of slavery, or it could execute a policy of consummate bluff, the consequences of which were even more forbidding.

The South chose the latter alternative and threatened secession. South Carolina's nullification had secured, in 1833, a compromise reduction in the tariff rates. Another compromise might be effected in the same manner. Bluff is an effective technique in diplomatic negotiation when the negotiators are few in number and capable of weighing the different aspects of probable result. But the technique is a boomerang where great numbers of people are involved. The northern citizen who rode into his village to vote for Abraham Lincoln on that memorable November day in 1860 was no more conscious of the probable outcome of his balloting than the southerner who cast his vote for Breckenridge. Each was simply registering his honest opinion and placing upon national officers responsibility for abating any threatened *impasse*.

When the secession bluff was called, the South became, even more than before, a section apart from the rest of the United States. Southern blood was spilled in defense of state and sectional loyalties, and the idea of section was thereby sanctified, just as the flag, Union, and the concept of individual freedom were rendered sacred in the North by the casualty lists of the war and the "waving of the bloody shirt" in the Reconstruction era. Thus, following the surrender at Appomattox, the main thesis of southern politics was loyalty to the "lost cause." The inevitable result of this spirit was the creation of a one-party system, for those who dared to vote the Republican ticket were stigmatized with treason to the South. The fact that the freedmen were generally Republicans contributed also to the creation of the exclusive hegemony of the Democratic party. And as soon as constitutional and administrative mechanics could be developed to thwart the plain intention of the fourteenth and fifteenth amendments to the Constitution, the Democrats were firmly entrenched.

The South did not, of course, participate in the election of 1864, but only Virginia, Florida, Mississippi, and Texas were non-participants in 1868. By 1872 there were no absentees.[17] As several of the states were administered by Republicans during the Reconstruction era, the two parties were very close in popular-vote totals before 1880.[18] In 1868

[17] Oklahoma is excluded from this statement, for it did not become a state until 1907.
[18] The southern popular votes for the four periods were as follows:

Period	Republican	Democratic	Others	Total
1868-1876	1,904,099	2,178,682	7,021	4,089,802
1880-1892	2,767,771	4,635,165	495,442	7,898,378
1896-1916	3,322,543	7,274,586	579,526	11,176,655
1920-1936	5,529,845	13,217,460	370,862	19,118,167
Total	13,524,258	27,305,893	1,452,851	42,283,002

the Democrats, by polling large majorities in Georgia and Louisiana, managed to secure a majority of votes in the section. However, the Republicans won North Carolina, Tennessee, South Carolina, Alabama, and Arkansas. Four years later, only Georgia, Tennessee, and Texas remained steadfast, the Republicans polling majorities in the other eight states. Majorities in these states gave the Republicans a majority of the section's vote. This was the first of the two elections in which the South failed to give the Democrats the usual majority. The second was in 1928, when the Republicans carried the section by a slight plurality.

Several factors contributed to the loss of the section in 1872. In the first place, the Reconstruction governments were retained by Negro suffrage and military garrisons. The Democratic party had no national ticket, in that it had only endorsed the candidates of the Liberal Republican party. And even though the official action of the party leaders was one of sincere endorsement, voting for a Republican, liberal though he might have been, was far from popular with the rank and file of southern Democrats. Many veterans of Confederate military service were still disfranchised. And finally, there existed in the section a general feeling of political futility; most believed that General Grant would be re-elected, that the Radical Republicans would again dominate congressional policy, and no matter how the South voted, neither of these facts would be altered in substantial detail.

In 1876, the Republicans held South Carolina, Florida, and Louisiana but, with no third-party votes the Republican share of the total vote of these states was but 50.9 per cent. In the other eight southern states, the Republican percentage was only 37.7 per cent. This election closed and sealed the

SECTIONALISM PREFERRED

Reconstruction era. Before the next presidential election, the Democrats were in power in every southern state. In the three elections of this controversial era, the Republicans polled 46.5 per cent of the popular vote, while the Democrats polled 53.3 per cent.

The "Solid South" emerged in 1880. From then to 1916, the Democrats carried every state in each of the ten elections. Not one southern electoral vote was cast for a Republican candidate. In only two of these elections (1884 and 1892) was the sectional score of the Democrats under the 60 per cent mark. In 1884 it was 59.4 per cent; in 1892 it was 55.1 per cent. The Republican percentage dropped under the 40 per cent line in 1888 and remained there except for its sensational recovery in 1928. For the ten elections after the Reconstruction era, the Democrats polled 62.4 per cent to 31.9 per cent for the Republicans. In 1904, their mark was 68.8 per cent and in 1916, 68.5 per cent. These were the section's high marks until the advent of the New Deal. In 1932, the South's Democratic mark rose to 79.6 per cent. From that peak it dropped slightly to 78.5 per cent in 1936.

The first crisis of Democratic leadership in the section occurred in 1892. Rapidly becoming a one-party section during the eighties, the logical result was internecine strife within the dominant party. The real threat came in 1892, when thousands of southern agrarians listened to the Populist call for reform. In Alabama, Georgia, Texas, and North Carolina, the revolt threatened the continued dominance of the Democratic party. Thus, at the Chicago convention the southern leaders were willing to pursue a policy that would reunite the party in their section. Thereafter the South supported Bryan with augmented majorities, even though the vote totals declined from 1896 to 1908 in each of the eleven states. In the former contest, the South polled 2,278,042 votes; in 1908, not counting the newly admitted Oklahoma, the total was but 1,634,618—a loss of 28.2 per cent—despite a population increase of 22.9 per cent. If the 1896 ratio of voter participation had continued to 1908, the total vote in the eleven states would have been 2,791,733, or an increase over the actual poll of 55.3 per cent.

The forced compromise of 1896 was a bitter pill for many Democratic leaders of the South. Thereafter, since most of the demand for intervention came from the lower economic groups, the conservative wing of the party began a systematic program of franchise restriction. In particular, the poll tax was used to reduce the political participation of these lower income groups.[19] But "understanding clauses" and the white-primary provisions of constitutions and laws were of major importance in reducing the number of votes. In addition, the consistent Democratic successes sapped the opposition of whatever hopes it might, in the earlier years of the Solid South era, have held for political success. Republican leadership fell, in many states of the section, into the hands of professional politicians who looked with disfavor upon a populous Republican party in their states. With national Republican successes coming with regularity, these professional Republican politicians found it easier to control the patronage if they had fewer eligibles for appointment.

In 1920, Tennessee and Oklahoma broke the section's record of Democratic consistency and there was a noticeable improvement in Republican popularity, but 1924 found the

[19] See Frank P. Graham, Barry Bingham, and others, *The Poll Tax* (American Council of Public Affairs Pamphlet, 1940).

SECTIONALISM PREFERRED

section again solidly Democratic, even though J. W. Davis's vote was less than that cast for James Cox in 1920.[20]

Governor Smith's nomination produced the last serious threat to southern Democratic supremacy. "Washing their clothes on the front porch" of Madison Square Garden in 1924, the national Democratic leaders had, for better or worse, challenged the defeatist attitude of the party and, especially, the right of the South to veto the nomination of candidates favorable to other sections. The southern leaders may have been firmly convinced of the effectiveness of their 1924 tactics in opposing the popular Smith. But the decisiveness with which the other sections sabotaged the candidacy of Davis was undeniable evidence that there was grave danger of another party arising as the alternative to Republicanism. If that were to happen, the South would be elbowed out of the national political picture. The success of LaFollette, without adequate finance or local organization, was a nightmare to Democratic politicians. Nostalgic for the days of Wilson, when they had "their feet in the trough," the southern politicians agreed to the nomination of Smith—Tammanyite, wet, and Catholic.

The nomination, even with the salve of Senator Joseph T. Robinson's (Arkansas) selection as Smith's running-mate, raised a storm of protest. Intolerant Protestants raised a hue and cry against Smith's church affiliation. Cartoons showing the Pope climbing through a ground-floor window of the White House were circulated through the section. Public opinion analysts have often-times pointed to this campaign as an example of effective propaganda. But, to the doctri-

[20] Davis increased the 1920 Democratic vote only in Texas, Oklahoma, Georgia, and Mississippi.

naires, the propaganda campaign of Bishop Cannon was not the determining factor. Opposition to Catholics flared throughout the section. Hundreds of thousands, as Simeon Strunsky has remarked, were waiting to strike a blow for God. These proponents of the modern Jehad were fired by the subconscious memory of the threat of Wallenstein's legions of the seventeenth century. Smith's advocacy of prohibition repeal was offered as evidence of moral depravity. As the South had not, in the past, fostered minor parties as mechanics for letting off steam, the anti-Smith elector was forced to vote for the Republican Hoover or to remain at home on election day. The latter was futile protest; the former untraditional. More than a million southerners smashed tradition, but the number who boycotted the election will never be known.

The Republican increases, phenomenal in many states, are shown in TABLE 3.

TABLE 3.—COMPARISON OF SOUTH'S 1928 REPUBLICAN VOTE TOTALS WITH THOSE OF 1924 AND 1932

	1924	1928	% increase over 1924	1932	% decrease over 1928	% increase or decrease over 1924
Virginia	73,359	164,609	124.4	89,637	44.9	+22.2
N. Carolina	191,753	348,992	82.0	208,344	40.3	+ 8.1
Tennessee	130,882	195,388	49.3	126,806	35.1	− 3.1
Total Upper South	395,994	708,989	79.0	424,787	40.1	+ 7.3

S. Carolina	1,123	3,188	183.9	1,978	38.0	+ 76.1
Georgia	30,300	99,369	227.9	19,863	80.0	− 34.5
Florida	30,633	144,168	305.3	69,170	52.0	+125.8
Alabama	45,005	120,725	168.2	34,675	71.3	− 22.9
Mississippi	8,546	27,153	217.7	5,180	80.9	− 39.4
Louisiana	24,670	51,160	107.3	18,853	63.1	− 23.6
Arkansas	40,564	77,751	91.7	28,467	63.4	− 29.8
Total Lower South	180,841	523,514	189.5	178,186	66.0	− 1.4
Texas	130,023	368,036	182.3	97,959	73.3	− 24.6
Oklahoma	226,242	394,046	74.2	188,165	52.3	− 16.8
Total South West	356,265	761,082	113.6	286,124	62.4	− 19.7
Total South	933,100	1,993,585	100.7	889,097	50.4	− 4.7

Amazing as the 1928 Republican vote in the South was, the controversy served to move many citizens to the defense of the Democratic party. In fact, the latter's vote was 1.8 per cent above that of 1924. The Republicans secured a bare plurality of the popular, and a majority of the electoral votes; but six of the states remained Democratic.[21] This election represented the roughest treatment that the Democrats had received in the South since 1872. However, the apostasy was strictly temporary, for the nomination of Franklin D. Roosevelt reunited the party into a more militant organization than it had been before 1928. Thus, from the point of view of party spirit, this internecine struggle was extremely beneficial to the party.

Middle West

Favored by geography and the political principles of the

[21] South Carolina, Georgia, Alabama, Mississippi, Louisiana, and Arkansas.

Northwest Ordinance, the Middle West, the very heart of the upper Mississippi basin, was destined to become the stronghold of agrarian democracy. Settlers poured into the rich agricultural lands of this section from the East, from the Border, and from the upper southern states. They brought with them the fundamental belief that ownership of property was a badge of respectability. In the circumstances of general equality there, the practice of universal white manhood suffrage became an accepted fact. And from that belief in equalitarianism, the section, even though a large proportion of its citizens were originally derived from the slave states, revealed an attitude opposing Negro slavery. The "underground railroad" kept its sporadic schedules through Ohio, Indiana, and Illinois, especially, and slaves were secreted to havens of safety farther north. In true frontier spirit, the general populace approved this open violation of the spirit of the Constitution and the letter of the laws. Even before the Civil War broke out, men stood solemnly in the public places of the Middle West and defended this sacrilege against the Constitution as upheld by a higher law—the natural law of human freedom and equality. The arguments of James Otis and other Revolutionary patriots were resuscitated from the memories of an earlier year. "Nature never made a slave."

In the period following the Dred Scott decision, sentiment in the Middle West crystallized rapidly under the leadership of men like Lincoln and Salmon P. Chase. The decision was bad law, remarked Lincoln, who was generally almost reverential in his regard for the Supreme Court. Since 1858, Lincoln had argued that the United States could not exist half-slave and half-free. And when the votes were counted in 1860, the Republicans had carried every state in the section,

SECTIONALISM PREFERRED

receiving 53.1 per cent of the popular vote to 43.3 per cent for Douglas's compromising northern Democrats.[22]

In the four elections of the war and Reconstruction years, the Republicans carried twenty-seven of the twenty-eight contests. Indiana's close vote for Tilden in 1876 marked the lone Democratic triumph. The party percentage ranged from 56.3 per cent in 1872 to 51.5 per cent in 1876.[23] Except for the unpopulous West, this section exceeded all others in its support of the Republicans in this first period. Only less than the Border was the Middle West torn by the war. Many had emigrated from the slave states in the *ante bellum* years, and they now found themselves and their sons in the Union army fighting against relations on the Confederate side. Especially in the southernmost counties of Ohio, Indiana, and Illinois the Copperhead (southern sympathizer) movement found numerous supporters.

Despite the war and the appeal to patriotism and flag, the Democrats showed considerable strength in the older states of the section. Even in 1864, they received 46.4 per cent of the Indiana vote. In the nineteen elections, that state presented the section's most consistent Democratic strength and

---

[22] Breckenridge received 1.9 per cent and Bell 1.6 per cent of the popular vote.
[23] The popular-vote totals for the four periods were:

Period	Republican	Democratic	Others	Total
1864-1876	4,501,143	3,681,780	70,276	8,253,109
1880-1892	6,784,922	6,146,832	626,758	13,558,512
1896-1916	14,614,685	11,826,428	2,641,868	29,082,981
1920-1936	29,328,525	23,135,716	3,495,842	55,960,083
Total 1864-1936	55,229,275	44,790,756	6,834,744	106,854,685

her 49.5 per cent in 1876 was the high mark of the party in this first period.

In the next four elections, the Democrats enjoyed greater success. However, except for Indiana's Democratic triumph in 1884, the Republicans made a clean sweep of the first three elections. Their marks ranged from 52.7 per cent in 1880 to 50.1 per cent in 1888. In 1892, the Republicans displayed their weakest drawing power since the war. Out-polling the Democrats (46.9 per cent to 46.3 per cent), the Republicans found that Populist competition was more favorable to the Democrats than to them, for the supporters of Cleveland gained one-half, while the supporters of Harrison were losing 3.2 percentage points. The total 1892 Republican vote in the section was twenty thousand less than in 1888; the Democrats picked up more then one hundred and twenty thousand, and third parties more than one hundred and ten thousand, votes.[24]

From 1880 to 1892, there was a steady decline in Republican strength in the Middle West: the Democratic fortunes were rising. However, the most important development in this period was the strength of minor parties. Their emergence coincided with, and resulted from, the rise of the industrial order. All of these minor parties—Greenback, Antimonopoly, Prohibition, Union Labor, United Labor, and People's (Populist)—pressed for increased governmental intervention. Their middle western vote grew from just under one hundred and thirty thousand in 1880 to 258,521 in 1892. In 1884, 1888, and 1892, third parties held the balance of power in the section.

[24] The Democrats carried Ohio (except for one elector), Indiana, Illinois, Wisconsin, and five of Michigan's fourteen electors. The popular vote was: Republican, 1,796,262; Democratic, 1,770,054; others, 258,521.

SECTIONALISM PREFERRED

The first four elections of the third period were disastrous to the Democrats. And not even in 1912 or 1916 did they equal their 1892 high mark (46.4 per cent). Fusion with the Populists substantially reduced the party strength. This diminution resulted from four prominent facts. First, the section's Democratic strength had since the war derived largely from small independent farmers who were still firm believers in *laissez faire* individualism; second, industry was moving into the section from the East, and any anti-industrial program would, therefore, meet the united opposition of all those engaged in it; third, a large portion of the electorate was still unconvinced that any good whatever could come from a Democratic administration, which traditional attitude had in no wise been altered by the two Grover Cleveland terms; and fourth, the Democrats were bad for national prosperity, inasmuch as the panic of 1893 had occurred during Cleveland's second administration. This last excuse for voting the Republican ticket was to plague the Democrats for thirty years!

With all these handicaps, Bryan was popular in the Middle West. Only in Wisconsin did his vote fail to surpass that of Cleveland in 1892. But the Republican accretions were phenomenally large. TABLE 4 shows the gains of the election.

When large numbers of citizens are, through fear of radicalism, moved to the exercise of their franchise privilege, the electoral decision is usually in defense of the *status quo*. Only in Indiana, Michigan, and Minnesota was the Democratic increase higher than the electorate's percentage increase. This must mean that, if most Populist votes went to the

Democrats, the voters added to the electorate were overwhelmingly Republican.[25]

The Democratic percentage slipped off almost a point in the 1900 election, but in 1904 it hit its lowest mark since the Civil War, and next to that of 1924, the lowest for the entire

TABLE 4.—NUMERICAL AND PERCENTAGE DEMOCRATIC GAINS IN THE MIDDLE WEST, 1896

	1892		1896		Per cent increase		Total
	Republican	Democratic	Republican	Democratic	Rep.	Dem.	
Ohio	405,187	404,115	525,991	477,497	29.8	18.1	19.2
Indiana	255,615	262,740	323,754	305,573	26.7	16.3	15.0
Michigan	222,708	202,296	293,583	237,268	31.8	17.3	16.9
Illinois	399,288	426,281	607,130	464,523	52.5	8.7	24.5
Wisconsin	170,846	177,335	268,051	165,349	56.9	−6.8	20.1
Minnesota	122,823	100,920	193,503	130,735	57.5	29.5	24.2
Iowa	219,795	196,367	289,293	223,741	31.6	13.9	17.6
Total Middle West	1,796,262	1,770,054	2,501,305	2,004,686	39.2	13.2	19.8

period. If the party leaders believed Bryan and the doctrine of intervention to be the causes of Democratic defeat, their alternative of Judge Alton B. Parker, the gold standard, and the doctrine of *laissez faire* proved to be a prescription worse than the disease. It produced voter paralysis! The sectional Democratic mark dived to 31.5 per cent. In five of the seven

---

[25] In Indiana, if the 22,208 Populists of 1892 voted for Bryan in 1896, if only the 7,468 Gold Democrats of 1896 revolted from the 1892 Democrats, and if one-half of the Prohibition loss went to the Democrats, the latter were only 18,906 short of their 1896 total. Giving them the other half of the Prohibition loss, the Republicans were 64,276 short of their 1896 total. If these speculations are at all correct, 77.3 per cent of the increased electorate in the 1896 election cast their ballots for the Republicans.

SECTIONALISM PREFERRED

states, the party polled fewer votes than were cast for Grover Cleveland in 1884, despite the tremendous gain in the electorate.[26] The Republican average catapulted to 61.8 per cent, highest in sixteen elections (1856-1916). For the second time in eight years, the Democrats had made a momentous decision. In 1896, they had invited Populists and interventionists into their ranks. When victory eluded them, they sought to return to their pre-fusion program. To win in 1900, they needed six hundred thousand extra votes in the Middle West. The return to the non-interventionist program in 1904 cost them a half-million votes, added over two hundred thousand to the Republican poll, and almost as many to the minor parties. The Democratic strategy might not have proved so disastrous if Theodore Roosevelt, the Republican candidate, had not executed the clever maneuver of promising governmental assistance in the smashing of "bad" trusts.

[26] The Democratic loss from 1900 is shown in the increase of percentage points separating their marks of 1904 from those of the Republicans. Thus, in Ohio, the Democrats were only 6.6 percentage points beneath the Republicans in 1900; but this gap was increased to 25.5 points in 1904 through the Democratic loss and Republican gain. The Democratic losses in the seven states were:

Percentage Difference

	1900	1904	1908
Ohio	6.6	25.5	6.2
Indiana	4.0	13.8	1.5
Michigan	19.3	43.9	29.5
Illinois	8.4	28.6	15.6
Wisconsin	24.1	35.2	17.8
Minn.	24.7	55.7	26.9
Iowa	18.6	32.9	15.1

PRESIDENTIAL ELECTIONS

The 1904 experiment was almost fatal to the Democratic party in the Middle West. Four years later, nomination of the twice-defeated Bryan was the only logical course. At least, he could revive the badly battered local party organization. In doing this, he boosted the middle western Democratic total by 533,650 votes, an increase of 37.8 per cent over the 1904 poll. From the point of view of the Middle West, this was Bryan's greatest race. In 1896, he had raised the party vote but 13.3 per cent. Yet Bryan's 1908 percentage (40.5 per cent) was his lowest in this section. Bryan's great contribution to American party history was that he dramatized the demand for governmental regulation of industry. The reaction of the separate states to the internecine Democratic conflict over intervention from 1896 to 1908 is shown in the following table.

TABLE 5.—INTERNECINE DEMOCRATIC STRUGGLE IN THE MIDDLE WEST
1896-1908

State	1896		1900		1904		1908	
	Pop. Vote	%	Pop. Vote	%	Pop. Vote	%	Pop. Vote	%
Ohio	477,497	47.1	474,882	45.8	344,940	34.5	502,721	44.9
Indiana	305,573	47.9	309,584	46.7	274,345	40.4	338,262	46.9
Michigan	237,268	43.5	211,685	38.9	135,392	25.8	175,771	32.5
Illinois	464,523	42.6	503,061	44.5	327,606	30.8	450,810	39.3
Wisconsin	165,349	37.0	159,279	35.9	124,107	28.0	166,632	36.6
Minnesota	130,735	39.3	112,901	35.8	55,187	19.0	109,401	33.0
Iowa	223,741	42.9	209,265	39.5	149,141	30.8	200,771	40.5
Total	2,004,686	43.8	1,980,657	42.7	1,410,718	31.5	1,944,368	40.5
Rep. Total	2,501,304	54.6	2,558,260	54.9	2,770,708	61.8	2,605,617	54.2
Republican Plurality	496,618	10.8	577,603	12.2	1,359,990	30.3	661,249	13.7

SECTIONALISM PREFERRED

As far as the Middle West was concerned, the Democratic *volte face* in 1904 was a particularly telling blunder. With an ever increasing demand for intervention, the party leaders turned their backs against the reform faction. The party lost face! For the next quarter-century, the Democratic party was hardly a factor in Michigan, Wisconsin, and Minnesota. The same decline, though in smaller degree, occurred in the other states. Having launched upon a liberal course, it was sheer folly, if not cowardice, to turn back in a moment of perplexity. And if the Republicans had not made mistakes of almost equal magnitude from 1910 to 1918, the Democratic party might well have disappeared from the middle western scene.

Theodore Roosevelt's 1904 gesture to the interventionists was more popular in the Middle West than in any other section except the West. Thousands of them remained in the Republican party and in 1908 voted against their former champion, W. J. Bryan. In 1910, they challenged the leadership of the Republican party. The Middle West furnished several of the outstanding Liberal Republican leaders, including Robert M. LaFollette, Sr.; Albert J. Beveridge; Albert B. Cummins; and J. P. Dolliver. In 1912, the section gave unexpected support to the Progressive party. Both Michigan and Minnesota gave pluralities to Roosevelt. The seven states contributed 1,339,566 votes to the Progressives, 1,150,086 to the Republicans, and 1,718,502 to the Democrats. Wilson received 225,866 fewer votes than Bryan in 1908. Only in Wisconsin, where the faithful followers of La-Follette sabotaged the Progressive cause, did the Democrats increase their 1908 percentage. The Wisconsin liberals firmly believed that their senator should have received the Progressive presidential nomination out of gratitude for his congressional leadership in the cause of reform, and when he was passed up in favor of Roosevelt many of them supported the Democratic ticket.

The neutrality program of Woodrow Wilson was popular in this essentially pacific hinterland, and the 1916 Democratic percentage was highest for the nine elections from 1896 to 1928. Through the nomination of Justice Charles Evans Hughes, a liberal statesman, the Republican schism of 1912 was substantially abated, though thousands of middle western Bull Moosers, the Progressives of 1912, must have voted for the progressive Wilson. The Democratic poll was 1,048,995 votes above that of 1912; the compromise program of the Republicans boosted their 1912 total by 1,878,624. In addition, the 1916 canvass was almost one and one-half million votes greater than that of 1912. There were too many factors involved to determine accurately the source of the tremendous increases achieved by the two major parties. Yet the election was much closer than the statistics indicate. Wilson carried Ohio, and third parties polled enough votes in Indiana, Wisconsin, and Minnesota to give those states to the Republicans by small pluralities. In fact, only Iowa gave the Republicans its usual preponderance of votes.

In the last five elections (1920-1936), Democratic fortunes in the Middle West have been very irregular. In 1924 they polled only 20.8 per cent of the vote, while in 1936 they received 56.5 per cent. The only other time that the party secured an absolute majority of the section's vote was in 1932 when 53 per cent voted for the Democratic-Liberal-Republican coalition of Franklin D. Roosevelt.

SECTIONALISM PREFERRED

The 1920 election silhouetted two of the chief convictions of the Middle West—isolationism and pacifism. This section lagged far behind the seaboard in generating enthusiasm for war against Germany in 1917. After the triumph, it had little desire to fulfill the logical responsibilities of victory. The Middle West viewed intervention in Europe as a twentieth century crusade, a meaningful gesture toward the stabilization of democracy in the world. But it had no disposition to fulfill the democratic aims through international legislative and administrative agencies. It was content to retire behind the geographic buttresses of that most impregnable section of this most impregnable continent and watch with a neutral eye the efforts of the world to govern itself along reasonable lines. Had not Europe been saved from a dispensation of force! Was there any reason democracy should not now operate successfully among the liberated peoples of central Europe? The Middle West, with the finest fabric of democracy in the New World, has never understood the failure of the free peoples of Europe to operate democratic systems. To it, liberty, and democracy are concomitant factors in the governmental equation and, if a people be really free, democracy is the inevitable consequence of that circumstance.

When Governor James M. Cox, a middle westerner, was nominated by the Democrats in 1920, he was naturally obliged to defend the Wilson administrations. The League of Nations was not popular in the section. A short while later "Big Bill" Thompson was elected mayor of Chicago and one of his chief sources of support derived from his opposition to the late and unlamented King George III. Twisting the British lion's tail was an effective political technique in this independent hinterland. The electorate showed its reaction to Wilson's international idealism by landslide support of the less international program of Warren G. Harding, of Ohio, and the Republicans.

In this first woman-suffrage election, the Democrats received but 29.1 per cent of the vote, the lowest mark since the Civil War. In Wisconsin, Cox received but 16 per cent of the vote, in Minnesota 19.5 per cent, in Michigan 22.3 per cent, and in Iowa and Illinois only 25.5 per cent. Even in Indiana, with the strongest Democratic traditions of the section, his percentage was but 40.4, while Ohio, of which he was a "favorite son," gave him but 38.6 per cent. The inexplicable feature of this result is that the Democratic administration had just completed a successful foreign war. But the innate pacifism of the Middle West reduced the Democratic party to its lowest mark in sixty years.

The "return to normalcy" program of the Republicans proved no panacea for the ills of a post-war world. Agricultural prices plummeted and the Middle West, essentially dependent upon farm products for its prosperity, became critical. The interventionist Liberal Republicans joined with the liberal Democrats in the investigation of administration scandals. Under the leadership of the veteran reformer Senator Robert M. LaFollette, the Liberal Republicans rose again to demand an amelioration of the party program so as to improve the lot of the common man. The militant interventionists were again on the march and LaFollette was personally popular in the section. When the Republican convention nominated President Calvin Coolidge, the liberal Republicans arose in indignation and launched the new Progressive party with La Follette and Senator Burton K. Wheeler, of Montana, as its candidates.

The revolt of the liberal Republicans left the Democrats in an unenviable position in the Middle West. Neither Governor Smith nor William G. McAdoo was popular there, and John W. Davis created no stir at all. He did not get into the line of fire, as the main struggle was between Coolidge and LaFollette. As a result, the Democrats received but one-fifth of the popular vote, their worst showing since the Civil War. The Republican percentage dropped from 65.3 per cent in 1920 to 57.3 per cent. The Democrats lost 8.3 percentage points. Only in the West did the Progressives receive a higher percentage of the popular vote.[27]

In early 1925 there was much speculation in the Middle West concerning party reorganization. The astonishing poll of the Progressives had reduced the Democrats to the rôle of a third party in this vital section. If the Democrats would fuse with the Progressives, as in 1896, there would be created a party that could fill the honorable rôle of opposition to the high-riding Republicans. The death of LaFollette left the

[27] The 1924 vote by states was as follows:

State	Republican	Democratic	Progress.	Others	Total*
Ohio	1,176,130	477,888	357,948	4,271	2,016,237
Indiana	703,042	492,245	71,700	5,403	1,272,390
Michigan	874,631	152,238	122,014	11,415	1,160,298
Illinois	1,453,321	576,975	432,027	7,744	2,470,067
Wisconsin	311,614	68,115	453,678	7,372	840,779
Minnesota	420,759	55,913	339,192	6,282	822,146
Iowa	537,635	162,600	272,243	4,037	976,515
Total Middle West	5,477,132	1,985,974	2,048,802	46,524	9,558,432

*These statistics, with but one obvious correction, are taken from *The World Almanac 1940*, passim.

Progressives practically leaderless and, as they had little local organization with which to carry the party through the period until the 1928 national election, the splendid promise of their first national race went to the grave with their dynamic leader.

With the passing of the Progressives, the Democrats again fell heir to their traditional task in the Middle West of offering an alternative program to the voters. Governor Smith's nomination was not displeasing to many LaFollette supporters. Though receiving as much as 40 per cent of the vote in but three states—Wisconsin (44.2 per cent), Minnesota (40.7 per cent), and Indiana (40.3 per cent)—Smith infused a new spirit into the Democrats of the section. His sectional percentage was 38.2 per cent to the Republican's 60.9 per cent. Smith's contribution was that of militancy. He exhibited a will to victory that contrasted strangely with the species of apology that had featured the Democratic pronouncements of the immediately preceding decade.

The tremendous popularity of Herbert Hoover in the Middle West reveals the popular faith in his ability to find solutions for economic ills. His support was more personal than partisan. He promised to apply his scientific methods to the loosening of the Gordian knot! But when the social engineer did little more than burn incense upon the sacrificial altar fires of Coolidge success, his popularity faded as has that of no other president seeking re-election. From a 2,575,247 middle western plurality over Smith in 1928, he dropped to 1,146,648 votes under the Franklin D. Roosevelt total of 1932. The percentage drop was from 60.9 to 43.8. Despite a 9 per cent increase in the section's popular vote, Hoover's 1932 poll was 21.6 per cent less than his 1928 vote.

SECTIONALISM PREFERRED

The economic debacle of October, 1929, produced the opportunity for merging the Democratic and interventionist factions of the Middle West. For the nonce, the ideals of nineteenth century equalitarian democracy were shelved in favor of Bryan's, Theodore Roosevelt's, and LaFollette's doctrine of intervention. Protection for private property, for equities in land ownership, and incidentally in industrial property, which depended upon agrarian markets, was the moral right of the government. The cycle from Hamilton, through Jackson and the rising agrarian democracy of the mid-century, had run its uneven course. Even President Hoover had moved toward governmental intervention, but his actions were too late, too hesitant, and too indecisive to satisfy the popular demand.

The election of 1932 brought the Republicans to their lowest mark since the Civil War, with the exception of the maverick election of 1912. In 1936, the Roosevelt coalition increased its 1932 percentage in every state except Iowa. And in Wisconsin, a state where intervention has long been regarded as a legitimate governmental function, the Democratic mark rose to 67.8 per cent. In Minnesota, with its Farmer-Labor traditions, Roosevelt received 61.8 per cent of the vote. Even in Iowa, the Democratic vote was 23,637 more than in 1932, but Landon's candidacy increased the Republican vote by 73,544 ballots.

The last two elections represent a major political revolution in the Middle West, for prior to 1932, the Democrats had never polled more than 46.4 per cent of the popular vote (1876 and 1892). The section's 1936 contribution to the total United States vote of the Democratic party was just under 30 per cent, which contribution was exceeded only

PRESIDENTIAL ELECTIONS

by the East with 31 per cent. The rise of the Democrats from the lowly estate of the 1920 and 1924 elections is shown in TABLE 6.

The political story of the Middle West is one of consistent Republican strength from 1864 to 1928. The Democrats

TABLE 6.—THE DEMOCRATIC UPSURGE IN THE MIDDLE WEST
(1920-1936) BY STATES

	1920		1924		1928	
	Pop. Vote	%	Pop. Vote	%	Pop. Vote	%
Ohio	780,037	38.6	477,888	23.7	864,210	34.4
Indiana	511,364	40.4	492,245	38.5	562,691	40.3
Michigan	233,450	22.3	152,238	23.4	396,762	28.8
Illinois	534,395	25.5	576,975	23.3	1,313,817	35.8
Wisconsin	113,422	16.0	68,115	8.0	450,259	44.2
Minnesota	142,994	19.5	55,913	6.7	396,451	40.7
Iowa	227,921	25.5	162,600	16.5	378,936	37.5
Total Middle West	2,543,583	29.1	1,985,974	20.8	4,363,126	38.1

	1932		1936		1920-1936	
	Pop. Vote	%	Pop. Vote	%	Pop. Vote	%
Ohio	1,301,695	49.8	1,747,122	57.9	5,170,952	42.5
Indiana	862,054	54.7	934,974	57.5	3,363,328	47.0
Michigan	871,700	52.3	1,016,794	56.1	2,670,944	37.9
Illinois	1,882,304	55.2	2,282,999	57.8	6,590,490	43.9
Wisconsin	707,410	63.4	802,984	67.8	2,142,190	44.1
Minnesota	600,806	59.9	698,811	61.8	1,894,845	35.6
Iowa	598,019	57.7	621,756	54.5	1,989,232	39.3
Total Middle West	6,823,988	53.0	8,105,440	56.5	23,822,111	42.2

occupied a distinctly minor position, even though, before 1904, they had never failed to command at least 40 per cent of the vote. Beginning in 1904, in only one election (1916) were they above the 41 per cent mark until 1932. And of the 133 separate contests in the nineteen elections, the Republicans won 105, the Democrats twenty-five and the Progressives three. Moreover, nineteen of the Democratic triumphs came in three elections—1912, 1932, and 1936. Thus, in the 112 contests of the other sixteen elections, the Republicans lost but seven—Indiana three, Wisconsin two, and Ohio and Illinois one each. Michigan and Iowa were the "most" Republican, Indiana and Ohio the "most" Democratic, and Minnesota and Wisconsin the "most" nimor-party states,[28] while Illinois was the most typical middle western state.

The West

The fifteen states of the West are not only a great geographic section of the United States, having just under one-

[28] The percentages of total votes (1864-1932) which each party received in each state are as follows:

State	Republican	Democratic	Others
Ohio	50.7	44.0	5.2
Indiana	49.0	46.9	4.2
Michigan	55.5	38.2	6.2
Illinois	50.2	43.5	6.2
Wisconsin	47.7	42.4	9.8
Minnesota	50.1	38.9	11.0
Iowa	53.4	39.6	6.9
Total Middle West	51.7	41.9	6.4

half the entire land acreage of the country, but they have exerted an increasing influence upon the outcome of national elections. In 1864, there were but four western states in the Union.[29] The block of fifteen states was completed in 1912 with the admissions of New Mexico and Arizona. In 1889 and 1890, six states—North Dakota, South Dakota, Wyoming, Washington, Idaho, and Montana were admitted. Utah entered in 1896.[30] Thus the West was an expanding section. In 1864, it cast only 3.7 per cent of the nation's popular vote; in 1936, that figure had risen to 16.1 per cent. And in the latter election, the section cast 16.8 per cent of the votes of the electoral college. The West can no longer be ignored, for it possesses political power of sufficient importance to merit attention by the leaders of any political party.

The political convictions of the section were largely derived from the Middle West and Border. Equalitarianism, individualism, and faith in democracy constituted its political trinity. During the Civil War and throughout the Reconstruction era, the West was the leading Republican section.[31] Not until 1888 did the Republican percentage drop below

[29] Kansas, California, Nevada, and Oregon.

[30] The other two and the dates of their admission were Nebraska, 1867; and Colorado, 1876.

[31] The West's votes by parties and periods were:

Period	Republican	Democratic	Others	Total
1864-1876	509,645	371,724	14,021	895,380
1880-1892	1,787,779	1,116,094	591,814	3,495,787
1896-1916	5,883,924	5,963,717	1,689,948	13,537,639
1920-1936	13,665,102	12,356,931	2,066,306	28,088,339
Total 1864-1936	21,846,450	19,808,466	4,362,089	46,017,061

SECTIONALISM PREFERRED

the 55 per cent mark. In none of the first eight elections (1864-1892) did the Democrats secure as much as 45 per cent of the vote. And in five of these elections, the Democrats were below the 40 per cent level. Nevada and California presented the greatest Democratic strength in this Republican era. In these first contests, Nebraska had an untarnished Republican record, while Oregon, Kansas, and Colorado present records of a single change to Democratic majority. Those with two Democratic triumphs were Nevada and California.

Western prosperity depended primarily upon agriculture, stock-raising, and mining. In the first two decades after the Civil War, the West was Republican for two principal reasons. In the first place, newly settled states and sections are usually nationalistic, or at least highly conscious of their patriotism. It was not fortuitous that the "War Hawks" of 1812 came from the newer sections of the country. Frontiersmen regard themselves as the vanguard of expansion and civilization. During this era, the Republican party had a practical monopoly upon American patriotism. The Democrats were anathematized as the party of rebellion. The second source of Republican strength derived in the West's conscious propaganda for improved methods of transportation. The citizens of this section wanted more railroads. The Republicans had consistently stood for national assistance in internal improvements; the Democrats were the party of state's rights. Republican administrations had fostered the construction of great transcontinental lines even to the point of corruption. Westerners cared little about who financed the railroads, and even less that the Wall Street corporations wormed the checker board land grants out of the politicians. The western citizen, no doubt, preferred that the roads be constructed without political corruption, but if there were no chance of getting the railroads without political corruption he would probably have still voted for railroads. None of the six western states voted for Samuel Tilden, the Democrat, in 1876. In fact, the West was less inclined than any other section to throw over the Republicans on account of the scandals of the Grant administrations.

Transportation was vital because the section was so far from markets, from the urban communities, and the eastern seaboard. There were cattle, sheep, and wheat, to say nothing of the machinery for mining and agricultural enterprises, to be carried from and to the West. Agricultural regions closer to the markets, seeking to capitalize upon their favored geographic positions, looked with a jaundiced eye upon the Republican sponsorship of western railroad building. This was one of the difficult issues which the Republicans had to compromise within their party program.

In the meantime, the mining and smelting of silver became a major industry in the West. When farm prices dropped, and freight rates remained high, there was a strong demand in the agricultural sections for governmental intervention in favor of agriculture. The panacea of soft money, of silver money, appealed to the citizens of the "Mineral Empire." If silver were placed upon a parity with gold, or if it were merely used as a common medium of exchange, western prosperity would be enhanced. Thus, the radicals joined their agricultural and silver policies to effect a solution for the economic ills of the United States, but especially of the West.

From 1876 to 1892, the Democrats remained near, though chiefly under, the 40 per cent mark. The real fluctuation

SECTIONALISM PREFERRED

occurred in the percentages of Republicans and third parties. In 1880, General James Weaver polled more than 5 per cent of the section's vote for his Greenback party program. With Cleveland running as a reformer in 1884, Westerners gave him no more support than they had given General Hancock, for Cleveland was not favorable to the West's silver policy. Both Republican and Democratic percentages slipped off in 1888. Third parties received almost 7 per cent of the vote. In 1892, the section vigorously revolted against both major parties. Only in 1912 did the third parties' percentage exceed that of 1892.[32]

The western Democrats were, in 1892, elbowed out of the way by the demand for governmental intervention. In the eyes of the malcontents, Cleveland was no more acceptable than the Republican Harrison; neither was an outspoken enemy of Wall Street. Westerners were rebellious against their colonial status. The rich corporations were the exploiters, exacting their pounds of flesh, impersonal, unconscionable, and pitiless! A farmer shipped his products to market, paid high freight rates and commissions, and got back a check far beneath his expectations. In addition, farmers

[32] The West's votes for six elections (1888-1908) were as follows:

Year	Republican	Democratic	Others	Total
1888	507,298	370,254	69,448	947,000
1892	557,721	232,280	474,894	1,264,895
1896	632,994	904,007	38,013	1,575,014
1900	877,985	790,701	44,335	1,713,021
1904	1,150,613	497,043	169,910	1,817,566
1908	1,133,722	850,514	149,347	2,133,583
Total 1888-1908	4,860,333	3,644,799	945,947	9,451,079

paid monopoly prices for eastern machinery and other equipment necessary for agricultural production. To these isolated Westerners, far from the market, it appeared that Wall Street arbitrarily set prices at both ends of the economic process, prices that would boost the profits of the corporations and reduce those of the farmers to a bare minimum. Would free Americans submit to this new form of human slavery? The answer of the Populists was an emphatic "no."

As the Republicans were in power nationally, the Populists naturally attempted to coalesce the opposition groups. In Kansas, Idaho, Wyoming, and Colorado, they formally took over the Democratic local party organizations. In North Dakota there was a Democratic-Populist fusion ticket, and in Nevada the Democrats were able to maintain but a skeleton structure. Only in California, the oldest state in the West, was the Democratic party able to maintain its formal party strength. As a result of this realignment, the Democrats, even in a year of national triumph, polled 37.3 per cent fewer votes in the West than they had polled in 1888, a year of national defeat. On the other hand the Republicans increased their poll by almost 10 per cent. The minor-party total vaulted from 69,448 votes to 474,894, a phenomenal increase of 569.4 per cent.

The Populists carried Kansas, Colorado, Nevada, and Idaho, and split the electoral-college delegations in North Dakota and Oregon. They only narrowly missed winning in Nebraska. Thus, in the West, the demand for fusion came from the Democrats and not from the Populists. The latter were riding the crest of optimism. Within a short while they hoped to wrest the control from the Republicans. The Democrats were already rendered impotent by the new crusade.

SECTIONALISM PREFERRED

The fusion of 1896 was, therefore, a surrender of the Democratic party in the West to the more numerous Populist element.

Though not immediately successful in the more populous sections, fusion captured the control of the West from the Republicans. For the first time since the Civil War, the Democrats carried the section. In doing so, they secured 57.4 per cent of the vote, reducing the Republicans to 39.1 per cent. The Democrats were to wait until 1932 before equalling their victory of 1896. Ten of the twelve states went for Bryan. Only in North Dakota and Oregon[33] did the Republicans capture the entire state electoral-college delegations. In California the Republicans dropped one electoral vote to the Democrats in a close contest in which the former out-polled the Democrats by but .69 percentage points, and in which third parties polled enough votes to determine the victor.[34]

In 1900, the Democratic vote was more than one hundred thousand under the 1896 total, while the Republicans increased their poll by 244,491. There were two important factors in this reversal. In contrast to the second Cleveland administration, McKinley's four years were indeed prosperous, and this tended to allay criticism in the agricultural stretches of the West. In the second place, this was a "khaki election." The United States had interceded, as it thought, to save the Cuban populace from the cruelty of Spanish military administrators. This country was protec-

[33] In Oregon, the Republican margin over the Democrats was but 2.11 percentage points.

[34] The Republicans received 146,688 votes to 144,618 for the Democrats and 4,579 for minor parties.

ting civilization and, incidentally, increasing its empire and influence in the family of Great Powers. Newer sections generally lead all others in patriotism. Frontiersmen are subjectively conscious of their historic rôle. "Teddy" Roosevelt, Republican candidate for vice-president, was very popular in the West. Hundreds of cowboys had joined his Rough Riders. On the other hand, Bryan had presented a very sorry spectacle, fighting mosquitoes in Florida while Roosevelt was storming San Juan hill. Moreover, Bryan ran upon an anti-imperialism program in 1900, despite his attempt, two years earlier, to lead a regiment of Nebraska volunteers against "Butcher" Weyler. The 1900 Democratic loss was greater in the West than in any other section.

The failure of the West, except for Colorado, Idaho, and Montana to support Bryan in 1900 may well have contributed to the Democratic nomination of Judge Parker. The leaders apparently interpreted the khaki election returns as indicative of a decided trend away from the doctrine of intervention. But the snubbing which Parker received all through the West proved beyond cavil that that section's love of flag was not synonymous with love of Wall Street. In every state, the party's vote declined. In North Dakota, Montana, California, and Washington, the Democratic percentages dropped below those of 1892. In the whole section, the party poll dropped from 46.3 per cent to 27.9 per cent. And, of most importance, those who quit the party went, for the most part, across to the Republicans in support of Roosevelt. The West was still interventionist, and the party labels of candidates were of relative insignificance. In each of the states, the Republican percentage skyrocketed, and some new highs were reached. The West led all other sections in support of

SECTIONALISM PREFERRED

Roosevelt. The Democrats were back where they had been in 1892, except that there was less hope, in 1904, of a future Democratic victory in the West. The Republicans had the voters. In eight years the Democrats had lost 30.1 percentage points. The losses in some states were almost unbelievable. In Nevada, the Democrats dropped from 81.2 per cent in 1896 to 33.7 per cent in 1904; in Utah, from 82.7 per cent to 32.8 per cent; in Colorado, from 84.9 per cent to 40.2 per cent; and in Montana, from 80 per cent to 34.7 per cent.

The last race of the "Peerless Leader" improved the Democratic position in the West. Colorado, Nevada, and Nebraska reasserted their faith in Bryan and the interventionist program. The party drew just under 40 per cent of the vote and the Republican mark was reduced from 63.3 per cent to 53.1 per cent. But Bryan received 53,493 fewer votes than in 1896, despite an increase of 552,044 in the West's popular vote. The uneasiness of voter affiliations was revealed in the third-party total of 149,347 votes. The revolters were to have their Roman holiday four years later.

The election of 1912 was not greatly different in the West than in the East, Border, and Middle West. The Democrats carried eleven of the fifteen states. New Mexico and Arizona were added to the Union in time to participate in the election. The Republicans retained only Utah of the ten states that were theirs in 1908, while California, Washington, and South Dakota cast their electoral votes for the Roosevelt Progressive ticket.[35]

---

[35] California cast eleven of its thirteen electoral votes for the Progressives. The popular vote there was exceedingly close, with 283,610 for Roosevelt, 283,436 for Wilson, 3,914 for Taft, and 79,201 for Debs. Senator Hiram Johnson, of California,

In no state did the Democrats poll a majority of the popular vote, the 44.3 per cent of Nebraska being the highest percentage for the party. Even for the three states that had gone for Bryan four years earlier, the 1912 Democratic percentages were from 4.4 to 6.9 percentage points lower. This reduced percentage resulted from the multiple choices of the campaign. Interestingly enough, Wilson polled 266,407 more votes than Bryan in 1908, 32,454 of which came from the two newly admitted states. Thus Wilson actually increased the Bryan total but 27.5 per cent in winning eleven of the fifteen states. Of the five sections, only the West and South gave Wilson more votes than they had given Bryan in 1908. However, the South boosted the Bryan 1908 total but 4,878 votes, or four-tenths of one per cent. This feature of the 1912 election is seldom mentioned. Both Wilson and Theodore Roosevelt were popular in the liberal West. Labeled as a conservative, President Taft received only 18.3 per cent of the total vote, which represented a 60 per cent reduction from his 1908 vote in the West. Even in the South, traditionally hostile to the Republicans, Taft received 15.7 per cent of the 1912 poll. And in the nation at large, his percentage was 23.6 per cent. This merely emphasizes the fundamental liberal tradition of the West, as well as its refusal to take the matter of party loyalty as seriously as the other sections did.

The election of 1916 was, popularly speaking, decided in the West. Democratic newspapers of the East had already conceded Wilson's defeat before the California returns were

---

was the Progressive candidate for vice-president. He must be regarded as a personal factor of tremendous importance in the Progressive poll of California and also of the entire section.

SECTIONALISM PREFERRED

complete. And when that state plumped for the President and against Hughes, Wilson's re-election was effected. As a matter of fact, the Democrats carried thirteen of the fifteen states, losing only South Dakota and Oregon. In no state did the Republicans receive a majority of the popular vote. On the other hand, Wilson polled 60.7 per cent in Colorado, 58.9 per cent in Utah, 57.1 per cent in Arizona, 56.8 per cent in Montana, 55.4 per cent in Nebraska, 55.1 per cent in Wyoming, 53.3 per cent in Nevada, 52 per cent in Idaho, 50.9 per cent in North Dakota, and 50.2 per cent in New Mexico. In the entire section, the Democrats polled 50.7 per cent to 43.5 per cent for the Hughes-Fairbanks ticket.

The key to this electoral decision was the failure of the Republican strategists to convince the Westerners of the genuine liberalism of Charles Evans Hughes. In California, for instance, the Hiram Johnson followers preferred Wilson to Hughes. The Republican leaders were plagued with the same party division that had beset the Democrats in the first decade of the century. The right and left wings of the party refused to support the candidates or the policies of the other.

Incidentally, this was the second time since 1864 that the West gave a majority of its popular votes to the Democrats. (The first had been in 1896.) The party picked up twelve and one-half percentage points over 1912. In Utah, this increase was from 31.5 per cent to 58.9 per cent, or 27.4 points; in Montana 21.9; Idaho 19.5; Wyoming 18.5; Colorado 17.0; and North Dakota 16.4. The decision was, of course, one in favor of isolation in American foreign policy and of intervention in domestic politics.

When the Democrats reversed themselves between 1916 and 1920 in regard to foreign policy, the West showed its indignation in an avalanche of protest votes. One can hardly believe that the West thought Harding a liberal comparable to Bryan, Theodore Roosevelt, or Wilson, nor did it regard Cox as less liberal than Harding. But the West did feel that national interests could be best protected by remaining as free as possible from European politics. The section's attitude was ably presented by Senators William E. Borah and Hiram Johnson.

Protesting this reversal in foreign policy, the western voters deserted their Democratic allegiance by the hundreds of thousands. Even with an increase of 174,932 in the total vote, the Democrats lost 761,442. Their sectional percentage dropped from 50.7 per cent to 29.1 per cent. Many could not go to Harding, so they supported Debs (Socialist) or Perley Christensen (Farmer-Labor). Third parties increased their poll by 91,824 votes. When the major parties fail to nominate candidates sufficiently liberal to please the West, the voters turn to minor parties.

The Democrats lost every western state in 1920. But the wholesale apostasy of party members was of more importance than the loss of the election. The Republicans won an absolute majority in every state. Only in 1892 and 1904 had the Democrats dropped below the 29 per cent mark. In North Dakota, the Democratic percentage dropped from 50.9 to 18.2. In Washington, the loss was 27 points, in South Dakota 26.0, in Colorado and Montana 24.8, in Nebraska 24.2, and in important California 22.4. The highest state percentage in the section was 44.2 in New Mexico, the lowest the 18.2 per cent in North Dakota.

If the 1920 returns were a deep wound to the Democratic prestige in the West, the 1924 election delivered the *coup de*

SECTIONALISM PREFERRED

grace. The party polled but 17.9 per cent of the total vote, lowest since the Civil War. The party leaders were demoralized. One cannot say that the West was particularly concerned over the deadlock at Madison Square Garden between McAdoo and Smith forces. But there is one thing sure— the western democrats wanted a liberal candidate. When John W. Davis emerged as the eleventh-hour choice of the convention, the West was definitely lost to the party. He wore none of the West's liberal colors and they treated him as they had treated Parker and even Grover Cleveland.

The LaFollette candidacy offered the liberal Democrats of the section a legitimate reason for kicking over the traces. In nine of the fifteen states, LaFollette ran ahead of Davis.[36] In two others, the Democrats narrowly averted descent into the minor-party rôle. In vital California, the Progressive ticket polled 424,649 votes to 105,514 for Davis; Washington gave LaFollette 150,727 to 42,842 for Davis; and North and South Dakota, respectively, gave 89,922 and 75,355 to La-Follette to 13,858 and 27,244 to the Democratic ticket.

The Democratic sectional poll was 27.7 per cent less than the party's disappointing total of 1920. In eight years, the party's western popular percentage had declined from 50.7 per cent to 17.9 per cent. This is plain evidence that the party affairs were not being directed in such a manner as to appeal to the interventionist elements of the Mineral Empire. And one can not logically contend that the Republicans, with Harding and Coolidge as candidates, were making any conspicuous gestures to this desideratum.

In 1928, the West received with increased favor the candi-

[36] North Dakota, South Dakota, Montana, Idaho, Wyoming, Nevada, California, Oregon, and Washington.

dacy of Governor Smith, but Herbert Hoover, a resident of the section, was naturally preferred. Despite Hoover's securing a majority in every state, and as much as 72 per cent of the vote in Kansas, the Democrats recovered a substantial portion of their late strength. In Utah, their mark rose to 45.8 per cent, while in North Dakota they received 44.4 per cent, and in Nevada 43.5 per cent. The Democratic percentage gains over 1924 were almost astronomical in states that had strongly supported LaFollette. The gain in North Dakota was 669.6 per cent, in California 482.3 per cent, and 277.2 per cent and 266 per cent, respectively, in South Dakota and Washington. Only New Mexico cast fewer votes for Smith than for Davis. Here the loss was seven-tenths of one per cent.

The effect of the Smith candidacy was, therefore, to rebuild the Democratic party in the West. Parties rarely spring to national success immediately following a crushing electoral defeat, and especially if the defeat is accompanied by disintegration of the local party organization. The campaign of 1928 gave to western Democracy the opportunity to build those local fences in every community. That the West, preponderantly agricultural, did not warm to the personality of the urbanite Smith is not strange, for Smith did not really warm to it. It was impossible for him to speak in language intelligible to the people of the wide-open stretches of the West.

The nomination of Franklin D. Roosevelt was particularly pleasing to western Democrats. Many of his most devoted pre-convention supporters, headed by Senator Thomas Walsh, of Montana, were from that section. The gentleman farmer, the country squire of Duchess County, New York,

SECTIONALISM PREFERRED

spoke as one of those who live on, and by, the land. There was an immediate personal tie that quickly destroyed their allegiance to the luckless humanitarian, Hoover. The depression had created a popular skepticism of the latter's ability to use his charts and figures to overcome the economic ills of human society. Hoover was a leader "of the head," Roosevelt one "of the heart," and in such an unequal contest the latter was naturally the fair-haired favorite of a desperate electorate.

Hoover carried each of the fifteen western states in 1928; he lost each of them in 1932. And Roosevelt's sectional percentage was but 5.4 less than the landslide mark of Hoover's 1928 triumph. In the four years, the Republicans lost 1,126,313 votes (31.2 per cent) of their 1928 total, while Roosevelt boosted the Smith poll by 1,941,825 (99.3 per cent). Third parties also picked up 196,163 votes. Only in Utah and Kansas did the Republican President receive as much as 44 per cent of the vote. The Kansas mark of 53.5 per cent was Roosevelt's low for the fifteen states. Thus, the position of parties was practically reversed in the West. One might describe it as amazing if he did not know with what ease this section changes its political complexion.

The success of the first New Deal administration was shown, in 1936, by increased popular support in all sections. This increase was especially noteworthy in the West. The 58.8 per cent mark of 1932 was boosted to 63.7 per cent. Only twice before had this section given a higher percentage of its vote to a party—1904 (64.5 per cent) and 1928 (64.2 per cent) —and on both of these occasions the Republicans were the favored party. Twelve of the fifteen states displayed their approval of the President with increased percentages. Landon increased the Republican percentages in South Dakota, Nebraska, and Kansas.[37] The Republican nominee was personally popular in these three states, as well as in neighboring Iowa, and he caught many 1932 bolters on the rebound.

In 1936 the Democrats occupied a position like that of the Republicans in 1928. One might be led to believe that 63.7 per cent of the whole popular vote would withstand considerable party adversity, but the 1928 Republican mark of 64.2 per cent dwindled to 37.4 per cent in the next election. This vacillating tendency of the West is, in fact, important in the forging of policy for the great parties.

From 1864 to 1936, the West cast 46,017,061 votes for presidential electors. Of these, 47.5 per cent were Republican, 43 per cent Democratic, and 9.5 per cent third-party votes. Of the fifteen states, only Kansas gave the Republicans a majority of its popular votes (53.5 per cent). Arizona and New Mexico were majority-Democratic states (56 per cent and 51.7 per cent); they were also the latest additions to the Union. Thus, for the entire period, twelve of the states gave only pluralities; in the Republican column were Nebraska, South Dakota, North Dakota, Idaho, Wyoming, California, Oregon, and Washington; in the Democratic column were Montana, Colorado, Utah, and Nevada, all prominent silver producing states. The three most Republican states were Kansas, California, and Wyoming; the three most Democratic were Arizona, New Mexico, and Utah; and the three most third-party were Washington, South Dakota, and

---

[37] In North Dakota, Landon increased the Republican vote by 979 votes, but the party percentage declined from 27.8 to 26.6. The favorite son, William Lemke of the Union party, was instrumental in increasing the total poll by 15,386 votes.

SECTIONALISM PREFERRED

North Dakota. The three nearest the section's party averages were Idaho, Nebraska, and Oregon.[38]

The Clash of Major Parties

In the preceding discussion, the political trends in the five sections have been followed. The differences among those areas present a recurrent problem for the leaders of a major party. TABLES 7 and 8 show what success the two parties have had in the nineteen elections. In TABLE 7, the forty-eight states are divided into quartiles upon the basis of their popular support of the Republican party.

In the first quartile are seven eastern states, bolstered by four states from the Middle West and Kansas from the West.

[38] The party percentages for the fifteen states for the entire period were:

State	Republican	Democratic	Third Parties
Kansas	53.5	37.9	8.6
Nebraska	48.5	43.3	8.2
South Dakota	45.3	41.6	13.1
North Dakota	47.6	41.2	11.2
Montana	42.1	47.9	10.0
Idaho	46.8	42.6	10.6
Wyoming	49.7	41.3	9.0
Colorado	45.0	46.9	8.0
Utah	43.9	49.5	6.6
New Mexico	44.9	51.7	3.4
Arizona	37.5	56.0	6.4
Nevada	42.5	48.9	8.7
California	49.8	41.5	8.6
Oregon	47.5	42.9	9.6
Washington	45.1	40.2	14.7
Total West	47.5	43.0	9.5

PRESIDENTIAL ELECTIONS

New England is here *en bloc* along with rock-ribbed Pennsylvania. Three states from the second quartile also gave the Republicans an absolute majority of popular votes. The twelve states of the first quartile cast, in 1936, almost one-third of the electoral college votes, as contrasted to the last quartile which cast only 28 per cent of those votes. And the top fifteen Republican states had 201 electoral votes to 145 for the fifteen least Republican states.

TABLE 7.—REPUBLICAN PERCENTAGES OF POPULAR VOTES, 1864-1936, BY STATES

First Quartile		Second Quartile		Third Quartile		Fourth Quartile	
1. Vt.	68.2	13. N. J.	51.9	25. Idaho	46.8	37. N. C.	40.4
2. Maine	59.2	14. Dela.	51.2	26. Cal.	46.0	38. Va.	40.1
3. Mich.	55.6	15. Ohio	50.8	27. Md.	45.5	39. Tenn.	39.0
4. Penn.	54.5	16. Wyo.	49.7	28. Mo.	45.2	40. Ariz.	37.5
5. N. H.	54.2	17. Ind.	49.1	29. Colo.	45.1	41. Ark.	32.4
6. Iowa	53.5	18. N. Y.	48.8	30. Wash.	45.1	42. Fla.	31.9
7. Kan.	53.4	19. Neb.	48.3	31. Ky.	45.1	43. Ala.	28.8
8. Mass.	53.3	20. W. Va.	48.0	32. New M.	44.9	44. Ga.	25.4
9. Minn.	53.1	21. S. D.	47.9	33. Utah	44.3	45. Texas	24.5
10. Ill.	52.2	22. Wis.	47.6	34. Nevada	42.5	46. S. C.	23.5
11. Conn.	52.2	23. N. D.	47.6	35. Mont.	42.2	47. La.	23.4
12. R. I.	52.0	24. Ore.	47.6	36. Okla.	41.3	48. Miss.	20.5

The second quartile comprises the remaining two eastern, the other three middle western, two Border, and five western states. Thus, the East and Middle West were exclusively in the upper one-half of the states, along with six western and two Border commonwealths. The upper one-half represented 57.4 per cent of the electoral college vote, a fact which is important in the explanation of Republican success since 1864.

SECTIONALISM PREFERRED

The third quartile is essentially a western bracket, with eight representatives. The Border had three and the South one. Seven of these gave over 45 per cent of their total vote to the Republicans. The lowest quartile has eleven southern states and Arizona. Even the latter returned that party victorious in three of its seven elections, but a greatly increased vote in the last two contests gave the Democrats a wide margin in popular votes.

The Democratic state percentages are shown in TABLE 8.

TABLE 8.—DEMOCRATIC PERCENTAGES OF POPULAR VOTES, 1864-1936, BY STATES

First Quartile		Second Quartile		Third Quartile		Fourth Quartile	
1. Miss.	87.4	13. Okla.	54.3	25. N. Y.	45.9	37. Mass.	41.4
2. S. C.	76.0	14. Ky.	52.2	26. Cal.	44.7	38. N. D.	41.2
3. La.	75.2	15. Mo.	51.4	27. Conn.	44.5	39. Wyo.	41.2
4. Tex.	71.0	16. Md.	50.9	28. R. I.	44.1	40. Wash.	40.2
5. Ga.	70.5	17. N. M.	50.2	29. Ohio	44.0	41. Penn.	39.8
6. Ala.	66.4	18. Utah	49.1	30. N. J.	44.0	42. S. D.	39.7
7. Fla.	63.9	19. Nev.	48.8	31. Neb.	43.4	43. Ia.	39.6
8. Ark.	63.8	20. W. Va.	48.4	32. Ore.	42.9	44. Mich.	38.4
9. Va.	58.2	21. Mont.	47.9	33. Idaho	42.6	45. Kan.	38.0
10. Tenn.	58.1	22. Colo.	46.9	34. Wis.	42.5	46. Maine	37.1
11. N. C.	57.5	23. Ind.	46.9	35. N. H.	42.2	47. Minn.	35.9
12. Ariz.	56.0	24. Dela.	46.3	36. Ill.	42.2	48. Vt.	28.5

The ranking of the states on the basis of Democratic vote percentages would naturally present an order generally in reverse of the Republican list. The first quartile states are all southern except for Arizona, which edged out the twelfth southern state, Oklahoma. All five Border states are in the second quartile,[39] along with five western states, Oklahoma,

[39] The logic of creating this section as a political entity would thus appear entirely justified. The spread of the Democratic percentage was less than six percentage points. It was almost seven percentage points in the Republican listing.

and Indiana. These western states are the ones that became Democratic with fusion in 1896, after which time they supported Bryan, Wilson, and Franklin D. Roosevelt.[40]

The third quartile presents five eastern, four western, and three middle-western states. These are the states that have been particularly vital to national Democratic triumph, because New York, Illinois, and California are in this bracket. States in the fourth quartile are of two types—die-hard Republican states and important minor-party states. In the former category are Maine, Vermont, Pennsylvania, Massachusetts, Michigan, Kansas, and Iowa; in the minor-party group are Washington, North Dakota, South Dakota, Minnesota, and Wyoming. The Democratic percentages of the latter are low because, when bolting the Republicans, the voters of these states refused to cross to the Democratic opposition; instead, they supported a Weaver, a Theodore Roosevelt (1912), a Christensen, or a LaFollette.

A comparison of the two tables reveals some important political facts. Fifteen states gave a majority of their total popular vote to the Republicans, while seventeen were majority-Democratic states. Thus sixteen states were mere plurality states. Yet thirty-one contributed as much as 45 per cent of their votes to the Republicans, while only twenty-five contributed a similar percentage to the Democrats. Thirty-eight were 40 per cent Republican states, while forty were in that class for the Democrats. The obvious meaning of these contrasting facts is that while the Democrats have a slightly more general strength in the entire United States, the Repub-

---

[40] Of the twenty contests involving the candidacies of Wilson and Franklin D. Roosevelt, these five states returned the Democrats victor in nineteen. Only Utah in 1912, by less than six thousand votes, spoiled a perfect score.

SECTIONALISM PREFERRED

licans have been consistently ahead of their opposition in the plurality states, i.e., in New York, California, Oregon, Washington, Idaho, Montana, North Dakota, South Dakota, Nebraska, Utah, Colorado, Nevada, Wyoming, Indiana, Wisconsin, and West Virginia.

CHAPTER THREE

The Minor Party Mission

THE contribution of minor parties to American politics is very generally underestimated or misunderstood. In a system characterized by two major parties, neither ideological in character, third parties become the natural instrument for those who desire to dissent from the major-party programs. But of more importance, minor or splinter parties, propagandist in purpose, serve to bring to the attention of the American public proposals that are too much in the nature of innovation, and therefore too radical, for either of the major parties to sponsor. Minor parties are the experimentalists of the American party system. They bear and nurture their progeny. Those who survive infancy and adolescence are induced by one or both of the great parties to bring their parents to a more pretentious domicile.

Fundamental alterations of the major-party platforms result from this adoption of minor-party policies. Plunder of splinter-parties is referred to as grass-roots determination of party program, but the important fact is that, if there had been no evangelical splinter parties to educate the rank and file of citizens, the grass-roots would have little knowledge through which to achieve program reform. Here, then, is

THE MINOR PARTY MISSION

part of the mechanics of American political progress. Neither of the major parties can afford to formulate an ideological program and thereafter to wait until the public becomes convinced of its practical merit. There is the job of governing, as well as the job of furnishing opposition to the government. These two functions are performed by the major parties. Government by formal party coalitions would have to be employed if the country were to depart from its historic party system. The minor parties, therefore, have become the agencies through which the public is prepared to accept changed political programs.

Since 1890, minor parties have performed this educative function with remarkable efficiency. A mature economic system presents fundamental problems of equality among citizens. In periods of expanding economic activity, political parties may, without immediate penalty, ignore pressing social problems, for the great majority of the citizenry is too engrossed with economic activity to give much attention to political issues. But when the economic tempo decreases, these social problems are magnified beyond their actual dimensions. America comes again to the crossroads. At least on three occasions she has come to that crossroads dilemma in the past fifty years—1896, 1912, and 1932. And when the country approaches the moment of decision, the work of the splinter parties makes its contribution to American politics.

Minor parties are important from another angle. They draw support from the voting public and thereby reduce the size of the major-party polls. Six of the last fifteen elections were plurality rather than majority decisions.[1] In each of

[1] 1880, 1884, 1888, 1892, 1912, and 1916.

them, minor parties had enough support to prevent either of
the major parties from securing a majority of the popular
votes. In 1892 the triumphant Democrats received but 46.1
per cent of the total vote, while in 1912 Woodrow Wilson's
poll was but 41.8 per cent. When the major parties do not
successfully reconcile their memberships to compromise
programs and do not, by remodeling their platforms, prevent
wholesale desertion to minor parties, there exists the possibility of a plurality election.

There were no third parties in 1864 and 1868, but in 1872
the Prohibition and Labor Reform parties made their appearance. Since that time, over fifty minor or splinter parties
have elbowed their way into the political scene. Of these,
thirty-five have nominated national candidates in one or more
elections. Others have done no more than hold conventions
and issue programs. The Prohibition party has offered a
platform and candidates in each of the last seventeen elections, the Socialist Labor party in the last twelve, and the
Social Democrats (Socialists after 1900) in ten.[2] Others of
the more permanent ones were the People's (Populist) party
for five elections, Workers' (later Communist) in four, and
National Greenback, United Christian, and Farmer-Labor
in three each. Moreover, some minor parties are federated
from separate state organizations. There may be even more
than one member organization within a state.[3] Two or more
splinter parties, *e.g.*, the Anti-monopoly and the Greenback
parties in 1884, may nominate the same candidates and the
same slate of presidential electors. The minor parties may

[2] The Socialists endorsed the 1924 LaFollette Progressive ticket.

[3] For instance, in 1912, the Progressive (Bull Moose) party had three Pennsylvania member groups—Washington, Bull Moose, and Roosevelt Progressive groups. See Robinson, *op. cit.*, 393.

also nominate the candidates offered by one of the major parties, as the Independent Labor party (Republican) did in 1888 and the Populist and National Silver parties (both Democratic) did in 1900. Or the minor party may endorse the presidential candidate of another party, while nominating a vice-presidential candidate from its own ranks, as the Populists did in 1896.[4]

Agrarian Protest Parties

The American minor parties may be classified into three general categories—agrarian protest, moral uplift, and industrial reform parties. The classification is by no means definitive, for some crusading groups might easily be included in either of two categories, while others, though not important ones, would fall into none. Moreover, some fifteen of the splinter groups have been of such negligible significance as not to merit discussion here.[5]

By utilizing considerable license in classification, one may find an agrarian-labor protest party in fifteen of the last seventeen elections. The march began with the Labor Reform party of 1872 and ended with Congressman William Lemke's Union party of 1936. Following the Labor Reform attempt came the National Greenback party for three elections. In 1888, the agrarian parties marched under labor titles—the Union Labor and the United Labor parties. In 1892 the People's party was organized, and it continued, though in a

[4] The Populists of that year nominated William Jennings Bryan for president and Thomas E. Watson (Georgia) for vice-president. Arthur Sewall was the Democratic nominee for the vice-presidency.

[5] For instance, the National Liberty and the Continental parties of 1904 polled only 830 votes, or one-sixteenth of one per cent of the total popular vote. One cannot say that these parties, since they immediately passed into the limbo of heroic attempt, left any very large impress upon American history.

practical state of political desuetude after 1896, until 1908. For the first election after 1872, the 1912 contest offered no agrarian or farmer-labor ticket. Most of the malcontent farmers apparently supported the Progressive ticket, but one may not logically classify that dynamic insurgence as even preponderantly agrarian.

In 1916 the issues were so vital as to discourage minor parties, but in 1920 the Farmer-Labor party made its appearance, polling the largest agrarian protest vote since the balmy pre-fusionist days of Populism. One may or may not include the LaFollette Progressives in the agrarian protest group. However, it was essentially a farmer-labor party and, for that reason, it may be included. Moreover, it did not derive from an organization schism, as did the Bull Moose party, and it reduced the strength of the Democrats much more than that of the Republicans. In both 1928 and 1932, the Farmer-Labor vote was insignificant, but in 1936 Lemke received almost three-quarters of a million votes, an agrarian protest figure that was exceeded only in 1892 and 1924. The popular votes for each of these fifteen elections are shown in TABLE 9.

The East has been poor recruiting ground for agrarian protest parties. In none of the fifteen elections has it led the other sections. During the period, the East had between 27.9 per cent and 31.6 per cent of the total population, yet only in two elections (1884 and 1936) did it give to the agricultural-labor protest parties support equal to the national average.[6] In 1884, the section cast almost seventy thousand

[6] The "national average" refers to the number of farmer-labor protest votes per thousand popular votes. The term "national index" is later used to refer to this national per-thousand vote average for the entire United States.

votes for Benjamin Butler, of Massachusetts, and his Greenback program,[7] while Senator LaFollette's 1924 Eastern vote derived largely from the support of organized labor.[8]

Being favorably located in relation to markets, the East's

TABLE 9.—AGRARIAN THIRD-PARTY VOTES BY SECTIONS, 1864 TO 1936

Year	East	Border	South	Middle West	West	Total U. S.
1872	2,981	5,919	6,809	11,554	2,236	29,499
1876	12,216	6,848	289	59,604	10,650	82,607
1880	47,441	56,652	50,960	124,649	27,877	307,579
1884	69,315	3,042	7,143	74,806	21,063	175,369
1888	8,382	20,127	40,349	36,622	43,581	149,061
1892	32,896	69,675	350,883	138,974	448,969	1,041,397
1896	461				25,331	25,792
1900	1,674	6,655	34,175	4,332	2,452	49,288
1904	13,373	7,076	43,712	16,576	32,133	112,870
1908		1,498	24,520	2,249		28,267
1920	38,176	4,753		86,613	150,457	279,999
1924	1,101,555	211,484	157,699	2,051,067	1,337,528	4,859,303
1928			1,283	3,068	2,019	6,370
1932				6,962	469	7,431
1936	214,155	15,072	3,173	401,429	91,686	725,515
Total	1,542,625	408,801	720,995	3,013,505	2,196,451	7,880,347
% Total Vote	1.50	1.15	1.71	2.82	4.77	2.36

farmers were relatively more prosperous than those of the other sections.

[7] The Butler strength came largely from the three populous states: Massachusetts, 24,433; New York, 16,994; Pennsylvania, 16,992; six other states, 10,896; total East, 69, 315.

[8] The LaFollette vote was as follows: Maine, 11,382; New Hampshire, 8,993; Vermont, 5,964; Massachusetts, 141,284; Rhode Island, 7,628; Connecticut, 42, 416; New York, 467,293; New Jersey, 109,028; Pennsylvania, 307,567; total East, 1,101,555.

This explains the negligible support given to the strictly agrarian crusades. In five of the nineteen elections, the section gave no votes to the cause, and in four others its support was under one-fifth of the national average. In another four, the section's contribution was under one-half of the national average. Thus, only in 1880, 1884, 1924, and 1936 did the East become very much interested in farmer-labor movements. And 92.9 per cent of its total vote for these parties was cast in those four elections.

Before 1896, the Border states were reasonably sympathetic to agrarian reform. From 1872 to 1888, these five states, led by Missouri, exceeded the national average in three of the five elections. In the last twelve elections (1892-1936), the Border exceeded the national average only in 1900. For the whole period, the section gave agrarian parties only 1.15 per cent of its total vote, making it the least sympathetic of the five sections to this class of minor parties. Even the LaFollette crusade failed to disturb its voter allegiances in 1924. Third parties have faced an insurmountable obstacle in the Border section because of the fact that the two major parties were of approximately equal strength; voter switches have been between these two parties rather than to the lunatic fringe. A voter could punish his own party leadership more by joining the opposition than through affiliation with a hopeless crusade. Moreover, intervention was not popular in the Border Marches until 1932.

The South presents a changeable record in regard to agrarian parties. During Reconstruction, the Republicans were the reform party in Dixie, but after the Democrats re-established their hegemony there, agrarian revolt flared until 1912. Discredited by a puerile record of achievement, the

THE MINOR PARTY MISSION

Republicans lost their reform leadership to the Populists. Almost every southern state developed an outstanding leader of the People's party, but those from Texas, Alabama, Georgia, and Arkansas were the most important. Beginning in 1888, the South exceeded the national average in five of the next six elections. However, the 1892 Populist vote of 350,883 remains the conspicuous agricultural revolt of the South. For the nonce, it appeared as though the Democrats might lose their one-party control of the section. Fusion preserved the one-party status, even though the Democrats had to compromise with the erstwhile Populist leadership and program.

From 1912 to 1936, the South spurned the agrarian crusades. For one thing, the mechanics employed to disqualify the Negro and the cumulative poll tax bars reduced the participating electorate of many states to small percentages of the population. Thus, the population strata that would have marched to the polls to vote for a Christensen, a LaFollette, or a Lemke found themselves unable to cast a ballot for any candidate. Franchise restrictions characterize this third period of no protest. However, the absence of protest votes does not mean that the citizens of the South were unanimously in favor of the Democratic party. It merely means that, under existing circumstances, dissatisfaction could be expressed only by undemocratic means, i. e., by economic pressure, by radical propaganda organization, and in many cases, by direct action. Another result of the conscious smothering of reform movements by the "respectable" elements of southern citizenry is that the preponderant Democratic party has experienced tremendous internecine strife, featuring the leadership of the "hill-billy Karl

Marxes." In other words, the abolition of separate radical reform movements has culminated in bitter internal Democratic politics.

Next to the West, the seven middle western states have most consistently supported the agrarian protests. Beginning in 1872 this section exceeded the national agrarian protest index in the first four of the six elections, and Streeter and Weaver polled sizable votes in the other two campaigns. However, from 1896 to 1916, the agrarian protest percentages were low in three of the elections and absent entirely in the other three. The section's earlier bent reappeared in 1920, when it gave Christensen 86,613 votes. In 1924, it gave LaFollette over two million votes, and in 1936 Lemke was the recipient of over four hundred thousand. In each of the five elections from 1920, to the present, the Middle West has exceeded the national index. Much of the section's prosperity depends upon agriculture, and there are no serious bars to divergent political action or to the exercise of the franchise privilege.

Of the 7,880,347 agrarian protest votes cast in the United States since 1872, the Middle West has contributed no less than 3,011,505, or 38.22 per cent. These figures reveal how important this section has been in retaining this means of more accurate expression of its citizens' political preferences. Thus, even though the East, Border, and South have collectively polled 69 per cent more votes than the Middle West, the latter section has contributed almost 13 per cent more agrarian protests than have those three sections.

The West consistently remained the foremost section in support of farmer-labor reform parties. Not until 1904 did the West poll fewer such votes than was her share by the

THE MINOR PARTY MISSION

national index. Bryan was sufficiently acceptable to draw the malcontents into the Democratic party. In 1908, the section had no Populist votes at all, even though three other sections cast 28,267 nostalgic Populist ballots against the then "not-so-young boy orator" of the Platte. And again, in 1932 and 1936, the Roosevelt candidacy satisfied those who might otherwise have supported the Farmer-Labor and Union standards.

Especially in three elections—1892, 1920, and 1924—the West far outdistanced the other sections. In those elections, the section's citizens cast a cumulative total of 1,936,954 agrarian votes, which represented no less than 19.65 per cent of the 9,855,982 which the section cast for all parties in those three contests.[9] And for the fifteen elections (1872-1936) the West contributed 4.77 per cent of her cumulative popular-vote total to farmer-labor third-party candidates. This percentage is 69.15 per cent above the Middle West's, 178.95 per cent above the South's, 218 per cent above the East's, and 314.78 per cent above the Border's mark.

The Prohibition Party

The Prohibition party is the principal representative of the moral-uplift crusading movements. Of all minor parties it has the longest continuous record, even though its vote totals

[9] The state totals and percentages of total vote given to agrarian parties (1872-1936) were:

North Dakota	144,330	8.61	Utah	37,137	2.41
South Dakota	147,871	7.63	New Mexico	10,647	1.38
Nebraska	214,158	4.51	Arizona	17,225	3.18
Kansas	359,362	4.90	Nevada	17,059	4.63
Montana	85,814	5.62	California	456,696	3.52
Idaho	64,680	4.83	Oregon	119,629	4.47
Wyoming	35,076	5.47	Washington	247,138	6.28
Colorado	142,723	3.82			

have not been so large as those of farmer-labor protest. From its début in 1872, it has appeared in every subsequent contest, and it remains today with a small, but exceedingly loyal, party membership.[10] It is interesting to look at the sectional aspects of support secured by the Prohibition party.

Though consistently unsympathetic toward agrarian protests, the East has continued to support the candidates of the Prohibition party. Not until 1904 did this section's Prohibition vote drop below the national percentage of Prohibition support though, except for 1920, the trend has been generally downward since 1896. The party was not able to increase its vote there at the same ratio as that in which the section's popular vote increased. Of course, after 1896, the Prohibitionists had to compete with other minor parties—especially the Socialists—for the support of those who couldn't conscientiously vote for either of the major parties. The section's peak was its 90,442 votes in 1892, from which it dwindled to its 4,367 low in 1928, a year in which an avowed eastern wet sought election to the presidency upon the Democratic ticket. Presumably most eastern Prohibitionists supported the "dry" Mr. Hoover, lest their support of the regular Prohibition ticket aid in the election of the "wet" Mr. Smith. The votes for each section in the seventeen elections are shown in TABLE 10.

The five Border states have given rather spotted support to the Prohibition party. In only two elections—1896 and 1928—did the voters of this section give to the party votes in excess of the national index. In the former year, the

[10] In two elections the Prohibitionists split into rival camps. Revolters in 1884 organized the American Prohibition party, while those in 1896 formed the National Prohibition party. Neither revolt was particularly detrimental to the party's strength.

Populist-Democratic fusion erased the agrarian protest party and some erstwhile malcontents must have crossed the Prohibition threshold. In 1928, the party's poll was the lowest

TABLE 10.—THE PROHIBITIONIST VOTE, 1864-1936, BY SECTIONS

Year	East	Border	South	Middle West	West	Total United States
1872	2,237			1,271		3,508
1876	4,243	892		2,678	1,709	9,522
1880	4,831	258	43	4,648	25	9,805
1884	65,184	9,080	6,136	58,386	11,567	150,353
1888	79,062	15,600	19,016	110,012	25,867	249,557
1892	90,442	19,360	15,165	110,717	26,313	261,997
1896	49,978	14,441	18,058	37,930	10,885	131,292
1900	79,700	15,732	16,505	81,436	24,691	209,064
1904	71,545	22,045	10,064	118,645	37,259	259,558
1908	75,262	19,200	7,545	107,116	43,353	252,476
1912	49,930	11,500	7,689	80,172	44,153	193,444
1916	57,598	10,571	10,861	77,059	63,968	220,057
1920	70,078	10,914	6,736	60,665	41,361	189,761
1924	11,442	1,418	6,198	15,786	20,925	55,769
1928	4,367	1,703		14,025		20,095
1932	13,401	7,023	4,979	42,879	24,568	92,850
1936	8,973	3,010	4,447	6,271	14,885	37,568
Sectional Total	729,273	162,747	133,442	929,696	391,529	2,346,687
% Total Vote	0.17	0.46	0.32	0.87	0.85	0.70

since 1880, but the break from it was less in the Border than in the South, West, and East.[11]

The South has come to be regarded as the Prohibition section, but its reputation did not derive from its support of the

[11] Varney polled but slightly over twenty thousand votes in the entire country, as contrasted to Faris's 57,550 in 1924, and Upshaw's 92,850 votes in 1932.

Prohibition party. In three of the fifteen elections (1872-1932), the party received no support at all in the South. In no election did this section come within 50 per cent of the contribution which it ought to have made according to the national index. Its highest percentage of national Prohibition vote—13.75—was achieved in 1896, in which year the South had 25.34 per cent of the nation's population. In 1928, Varney received no votes in the South, for with Smith running as the candidate of the dominant Democratic party, the Prohibitionists realized that a vote for Varney was in reality a vote for Smith, the wet. The largest southern Prohibition party vote was 19,016 in 1888, but it must be remembered that the southern vote of that period was larger than for two decades after the turn of the century. That is the price that the section paid for disfranchising the Negro and the submerged white groups.

The Middle West has been the most consistent supporter of the Prohibitionists since the party's inception. In every election, the section's contribution has far exceeded the national index. In ten of those contests the section has exceeded the index mark by 40 per cent. In 1928 almost 70 per cent of Varney's small total came from the enduring Prohibition organization of that politically-minded section. The LaFollette campaign cut the party's vote to almost one-fourth of the 1920 total. The first Bryan campaign reduced the 1892 total by 65.8 per cent. This is illustrative of the effect which a major, or even a minor, party reorganization may have upon the fortunes of third parties.

The West's Prohibition record is inconsistent, as contrasted with both the East and Middle West. Though missing but two of the sixteen elections (1872-1932), the section at no

THE MINOR PARTY MISSION

time gave the party's leaders much reason for optimism. It failed to poll any Prohibition votes in 1872 and 1928 and was below the index mark in 1880 and 1896. The West's interest in Prohibition could not compare with that in agrarian reform, as the latter was above the index in nine elections and the Prohibitionists in only seven. However, in three of these seven, the agrarians had no third party in the field. In the elections in which both groups had candidates the agrarians led seven to four. In total votes the agrarians were far ahead—2,196,451 to 356,664. In other words, from 1872-1936, the Prohibition vote total was but 16.94 per cent of the West's agrarian total.

Of the entire United States, the states having the highest percentage of Prohibition votes were California and Florida, but the middle western states were, as a group, ahead of any other section. All seven were in the highest twenty states, and five in the first twelve. Seven of the eastern states were in the upper one-half of the states. Seven of the West's fifteen states were also in that bracket. Six southern and six western states were in the lowest twelve.

Industrial Reform Parties

The reformation of the industrial order became, after the passing of the agricultural frontier in the late eighties, the avowed purpose of several minor parties. The farmer-labor movements were largely imbued with the principles of nineteenth century progressivism, i.e. that the government should intervene to equalize opportunity between the great corporations and millionaires on the one hand and the common citizens and have-nots on the other. "Equality of opportuni-

121

ty" was an omnipresent slogan. Nevertheless, even in a system of governmental regulation, the progressives hoped to retain private property and business competition.

The industrial reformists expressed contempt for such roseate hopes. The only procedure for maintaining individual equality was to nationalize industrial property. They drew their inspiration from the Marxist doctrines of German socialism, and especially from the Erfurt Program. The Socialist Labor party made its first national campaign in 1892, polling 21,532 votes in seven states.[12] From that original entry, the party has nominated candidates in each of the subsequent campaigns. Though utterly insignificant in volume, the party vote has never dropped below 12,777 (1936) and has never risen above 38,958 (1924). In eleven elections (1892-1932), the party's votes totaled 288,451, of which 55.1 per cent came from the East, and 26.2 per cent from the Middle West. Thus, only 18.7 per cent of the Socialist Labor vote derived in the thirty-two states of the other three sections. Support of such a radical program would necessarily be restricted to the important industrial states.[13]

In 1900, the Social Democratic party made its appearance in national politics. Its organizers were the more conservative of the radical Socialist Labor party of the preceding decade.[14] Though anticipating the future nationalization of

[12] New York, 17,956; New Jersey, 1,337; Pennsylvania, 898; Massachusetts, 649; Maine, 336; Connecticut, 329; and Maryland, 27. Stanwood, *op. cit.*, I, 517.

[13] Eight states of the East and Middle West contributed 65.4 per cent of the total Socialist Labor vote. The individual state contributions, in percentage, were: New York, 27.6 per cent; Illinois, 8.9 per cent; Massachusetts, 6.6. per cent; Michigan, 5.3 per cent; New Jersey, 5 per cent; Ohio, 4.7 per cent; and Indiana and Connecticut, 3.7 per cent each. In none of these states, however, was the party's vote a significant portion of the total popular vote.

[14] The split in the Socialist Labor ranks did not result in a loss of votes for the parent party, as it polled over one thousand more votes in 1900 than in 1896.

THE MINOR PARTY MISSION

property, the new party expressed the hope that such transition to Socialism could be achieved gradually and by evolutionary, instead of revolutionary, tactics. Eugene V. Debs, who became a labor martyr in the famous Pullman strike, was nominated for the presidency in this initial campaign. He was the party candidate in five elections. His last race (1920) was one of his best despite his being incarcerated in the federal prison at Atlanta for opposition to American participation in the World War.

Except for 1924, when they endorsed the LaFollette Progressive ticket, the Socialists have contested every election since their inception. And during that period they have been the most important permanent minor party in American politics. They led all minor parties in 1904, 1908, 1916, 1920, 1928, and 1932, being outvoted by the Prohibitionists in 1900, the Bull Moose Progressives in 1912, and the Lemke Unionists in 1936.[15] In their nine campaigns, the Socialists have amassed a total of 5,080,825 popular votes, or 40.3 per cent of the entire minor party roll for those elections.

The Socialist votes have come from two principal sources —industrial workers and disgruntled agriculturists. Trade unionists of the East and Middle West have remained the backbone of this movement, as in Great Britain and other countries of western Europe, but after the failure of the fusion with the Democrats to effect the realization of Populist dreams, thousands of agrarian crusaders supported Debs and his rather mild socialistic program. Before the war, this backwash of Populism was a most vital source of Socialist strength.

[15] They would certainly have been outvoted by the LaFollette Progressives in 1924 but for their joining them during the campaign.

PRESIDENTIAL ELECTIONS

In order to present more graphically the geographic aspects of Socialist strength for the nine elections, the states have been classified according to the percentage of total votes which each has cast for the Socialist party. The election of 1924 was excluded from this analysis.

TABLE II.—SOCIALIST PERCENTAGES OF TOTAL VOTE 1900-1936

First Quartile		Second Quartile		Third Quartile		Fourth Quartile	
1. Wis.	4.64	13. Colo.	2.27	25. Texas	1.54	37. Miss.	.93
2. Nevada	4.61	14. Kan.	2.25	26. Ark.	1.51	38. Ala.	.76
3. Okla.	4.21	15. Ill.	2.21	27. S. D.	1.49	39. N. H.	.74
4. N. Y.	4.15	16. N. D.	2.16	28. Wyo.	1.45	40. La.	.69
5. Wash.	3.64	17. Ohio	2.15	29. Ia.	1.45	41. Dela.	.65
6. Mont.	3.47	18. Fla.	2.14	30. Ind.	1.39	42. Ken.	.60
7. Oregon	3.45	19. Conn.	2.10	31. W. Va.	1.37	43. R. I.	.59
8. Cal.	3.37	20. Idaho	2.01	32. Vt.	1.16	44. Tenn.	.51
9. Mo.	3.16	21. Mass.	1.64	33. Ariz.	1.15	45. Va.	.30
10. Minn.	3.07	22. Mich.	1.63	34. Md.	1.05	46. Ga.	.25
11. Penn.	2.61	23. N. J.	1.61	35. New M.	1.05	47. N. C.	.20
12. Utah	2.56	24. Neb.	1.55	36. Maine	.98	48. S. C.	.09

The prominent rôle of the former Populist states in this percentage ranking is quickly discernible. Of those in the upper quartile only New York and Pennsylvania had been unmoved by that agrarian revolt. At least sixteen of the first twenty-four states were Populist strongholds in the nineties. Though not in the Union during the Populist era, Oklahoma is a good example of the turn from Populism to Socialism. In her first three elections (1908, 1912, and 1916), Oklahoma cast 14 per cent of her total vote for the Socialist ticket,[16] but Nevada had 10.9 per cent, Washington 8.8 per

[16] There were other factors besides tenant farming and low agricultural income, for the Negroes, abandoned by "lily-white" Republican leaders, supported the Socialists.

THE MINOR PARTY MISSION

cent, Montana 8.1 per cent, and Idaho 8 per cent. The fact is that thousands of erstwhile Populists, though probably supporting fusion in good faith, lost hope in the Democratic party when Alton B. Parker was nominated in 1904. They remained staunch believers in intervention, and though it is doubtful that they would have approved nationalization of all property, they nevertheless supported the principle in regard to railroads and banks.

Of the five sections, the East has been most favorable to the Socialists, both in votes and in party percentage of total popular votes. Its 1,910,096 Socialist votes constituted 2.8 per cent of its total vote in the nine elections. However, only New York with its 1,060,926 Socialist votes, and its 4.15 per cent was above the sectional average. Only New York and Pennsylvania were above the national Socialist percentage mark. The eastern Socialist strength was largely derived from industrial workers.

The West, with six states in the upper quartile, and eleven of its fifteen states in the upper half, contributed 960,288 votes for a Socialist record of 2.71 per cent. Nevada, Washington, Montana, Oregon, and California were above the West's average, but Utah and Colorado were also above the United States average. No western state was in the lowest quartile. The Socialist strength in this section came largely from disillusioned former Populists and from miners, lumbermen, and maritime workers.

Next to the East, the Middle West gave the Socialists the largest block of votes—1,580,406—but the section's average was only 2.23 per cent. From 1904 to 1920, it contributed more votes to the party than any other section. Wisconsin and Minnesota were in the upper quartile, and Illinois, Ohio, and Michigan in the second. Industrial workers were the greatest source of Socialist strength there, but former agrarian radicalism was important in Michigan, Wisconsin, and Minnesota.

The Border and South were the least favorable to the party. Third parties generally experienced difficulty in acquiring a foothold in the Border, though Missouri was a noteworthy exception. Missouri cast 57.8 per cent of the Border's Socialist vote, making her the section's only state above the national average. Nostalgia for the Populist program was the chief source of Socialist strength there. The coal miners of West Virginia placed that state above the section's average, but Delaware and Kentucky, both strong two-party states, and anti-interventionist, were conspicuously low. Socialist strength has since 1916 increased in Maryland.

Little need be said about the Socialist strength in the South. Eight of its twelve states were in the lowest quartile, and two others, Texas and Arkansas, in the third. Though participating in but seven of the nine elections, Oklahoma contributed 43.7 per cent of the South's total Socialist vote. Florida was the only other member of the section in the upper one-half of the states.[17] The voting restrictions and political habits of the South do not contribute to the existence of third parties, especially those with radical economic programs.

[17] In Florida, the Republican party was very anemic from 1892 to 1924, which left a better opportunity for the Socialists to exist as a separate party. From 1900 to 1920, the Socialists won 22,027 votes to 90,025 for the Republicans, or 19.7 per cent of the Republican-Socialist total. Even in Oklahoma, with its large Socialist vote during this period, that party accounted for but 19.8 per cent of the Republican-Socialist total.

THE MINOR PARTY MISSION

Sectional Aspects of Minor Party Strength

It would be helpful to study briefly the complete picture of minor-party activity in national elections. As has been noted, the Prohibition vote was largely from the Middle West and the East, the agrarian protest strength was essentially from the West, the Middle West, and before 1896, the South, and the Socialist support primarily from the West, Middle West, and East. The Border was hostile ground to all minor parties, and the South became even more so after 1900, when suffrage restrictions became effective in that preponderantly Democratic section.

In the nineteen elections, a total of 20,017,949 votes were cast for minor parties. Of course, there were scattering ballots that were not reported in any of the official returns. Election officials use their discretion in reporting senseless votes.[18] No doubt, where votes are so few in number as not to influence the election or add to the prestige of a party, many are never included in the final tabulations.[19]

In TABLE 12, the states are ranked and listed according to the percentage of total votes which they cast for minor parties.

The minor-party mark for the United States was 5.7 per cent. Pennsylvania was the average state, with nineteen above and twenty-eight below her. The first nineteen states are all in that section which stretches west and southwest

[18] For instance, South Carolina reported one vote for Andrew Gump in 1924, despite the fact that that fictitious character was not a serious candidate for the presidency except in the fertile imagination of his creator, Sidney Smith.

[19] Even the meticulous Professor E. E. Robinson, after trying to interpret the official state records, in many instances merely lists insignificant blocks of votes as "scattering."

from Lake Huron, including five states of the Middle West and all of the West except New Mexico. These nineteen states comprise the great Upper Mississippi Basin, with its wheat, corn, pork and dairy industries, and the Mineral Empire with its enduring sectional policy on silver and transportation. Only Minnesota and Wisconsin, proudly conscious third-party states with their Progressive and Farmer-Labor political propensities, intrude upon what would other-

TABLE 12.—STATE PERCENTAGES OF TOTAL VOTES CAST FOR MINOR PARTIES, 1864-1936

First Quartile		Second Quartile		Third Quartile		Fourth Quartile	
1. Wash.	14.7	13. Neb.	8.2	25. Texas	4.5	37. N. M.	3.4
2. S. D.	12.4	14. Colo.	8.0	26. Okla.	4.3	38. Conn.	3.3
3. N. D.	11.2	15. Ia.	6.9	27. Fla.	4.3	39. Vt.	3.2
4. Minn.	11.0	16. Utah	6.5	28. N. J.	4.2	40. Tenn.	2.8
5. Idaho	10.6	17. Ariz.	6.5	29. Ga.	4.1	41. Ken.	2.7
6. Mont.	10.0	18. Mich.	6.2	30. Ind.	4.0	42. N. H.	2.6
7. Wis.	9.9	19. Ill.	6.2	31. R. I.	3.9	43. Del.	2.5
8. Ore.	9.5	20. Penn.	5.7	32. Ark.	3.8	44. Miss.	2.2
9. Cal.	9.3	21. N. Y.	5.4	33. Maine	3.7	45. N. C.	2.1
10. Wyo.	9.0	22. Mass.	5.4	34. Md.	3.6	46. Va.	1.7
11. Nevada	8.7	23. Ohio	5.2	35. W. Va.	3.6	47. La.	1.3
12. Kan.	8.6	24. Ala.	4.8	36. Mo.	3.5	48. S. C.	.6

wise have been an exclusive western collection of first-quartile states. As it was, these two crowded out Nebraska and Colorado by less than one percentage point. The high western marks, topped by the 14.7 per cent of Washington, were the result of support given to the Populists, the 1912 Progressives, the Christensen Farmer-Labor party of 1920, the LaFollette-Wheeler ticket of 1924, the Lemke Union party of 1936, and the Socialists for their nine campaigns.

THE MINOR PARTY MISSION

The second quartile states comprise four each from the West and Middle West, three from the East, and Alabama from the South. These middle-western states supported most of the third-party movements, but the largest votes were rolled up for the Progressive parties of 1912 and 1924. The three most populous eastern states likewise gave strong support to the Progressive causes, but they, being industrial states, have also backed the industrial reform parties.

Except for Alabama in the second, the strongly Populist southern states are in the third quartile. Most of their third-party vote was amassed during that era. The Border states fall in a clump at the bottom of the third and the top of the fourth quartiles. In political behavior, they have had greater consistency than either the East or the South.

The last quartile comprises states in which the two major parties divide the electorate on quite even terms or in which the dominant party has, by legal mechanics and propaganda, rendered public support of a radical party a difficult if not impossible privilege. The last five states utilized the poll-tax franchise requirement to reduce the number of participants who might be expected to become enamoured of the promises of the lunatic fringe, though two of them have recently abandoned that technique.

The minor-party marks were: West, 9.5 per cent; Middle West, 6.4 per cent; East, 5.1 per cent; Border, 3.3 per cent; and South, 3.2 per cent. Of the more than twenty million third-party votes, the farmer-labor parties account for 39.4 per cent, the Socialists for 23.3 per cent, the 1912 Progressives for 20.6 per cent, the Prohibitionists for 11.2 per cent, and the multitude of other splinter groups for the remaining 5.5 per cent.

As a result of the foregoing discussion, it is evident that, though the American political party system is usually regarded as a two-party system, this is true only in consideration of the country as a whole. In the extreme South, a one-party system has prevailed since the turn of the century, except for the election of 1928 when the Democratic split gave the Republican ticket (but not the Republicans) a sectional majority; in the Border and most of the East and Middle West, the major parties dominate; but in the mercurial West, party allegiances are so impermanent as to present a practical multi-party system. Moreover, the example of the West appears to be spreading to other sections, except the South, and national leaders of the major parties may find it increasingly difficult to compromise the great differences that exist among the geographic regions as well as the conflicts that plague those seeking peaceful relations within the industrial order. The achievement of such compromises within a single political party program is an act of consummate statesmanship in these times of hair-trigger economics, of international nervousness, and of traditional social mores. On account of these new conflicting factors, the modern major parties are quite different organizations from those which fought for the control of the national government before 1896. The development of Populism in the early nineties, reflecting the contradictions of the American economic system, ushered in this new political order. An honest evaluation of minor parties should not be that they are intruders in sacred precincts, but that they are the only democratic means by which the American people can retain the system of two great major parties and at the same time reach for solutions of emergent political problems. The major parties will probably become more ethereal in statement of principles as the difficulty of group reconciliation increases, and minor parties will continue their faithful rôle of educating the electorate on the questions that are of necessity ignored by both major parties.

Contributions of Minor Parties

In this essentially two-party system, minor parties have made their contribution to American political history through channels other than election of their own candidates to office. From that historic first decade of the nineteenth century, when the querulous John Randolph railed at President Jefferson's abandonment of campaign promises, to the election of 1936, only one minor party has succeeded in intruding itself into the two-party system. This was the Republican party. It achieved that important status in six years. But the political conditions of that rise were distinctly abnormal. In their zeal to compromise the sectional views on slavery, the Whigs, through dilution of program, lost the allegiance of former party members. From 1852 to the Civil War, the Whig party was little more than a group of leaders in search of voting legions. They never found them. Thousands of erstwhile Whigs joined the Know-nothing party in the middle fifties and crossed to the new Republican standard before 1860. Thus, contrary to some opinion, the Republicans did not usurp the place of the Whigs. The Whigs had no place. The Republicans merely moved into a vacancy which, no doubt, might have come into the possession of the Know-nothing party if its program had been sufficiently realistic to meet the issues of that presageful period.

The exigencies of day-by-day government and opposition

require that the two large parties live in the present. Neither can afford to push itself very far in advance of public thinking. Intellectuals are notoriously critical of party leaders for failure to pledge their parties to long-range programs. But intellectuals fail to realize that the leaders must marshal the rank and file of American citizens into effective political bodies. They cannot risk the hazard of immediate defeat. Future party policy must, therefore, be sacrificed to the demands of the present.

This luxury of pursuing an idealistic course is the special privilege of minor parties. They have not the weight of members who seek immediate desiderata. When the Prohibition party entered the field in the late sixties of last century, the promise of immediate success was certainly not bright. Its members were sacrificing any influence they might have exerted upon the existing political situation for the promise of ultimate victory. They consciously chose an educative, propagandist, and idealistic course. They focused attention upon a great social problem and, although the Anti-Saloon League, a nonpartisan pressure group, was more important in creating the conditions out of which came the "noble experiment," their efforts and faith were rewarded in the adoption of the reform for which they had fought for more than half a century.

The Socialist-Labor, the Socialist, and the Communist parties have likewise pursued such propagandist course. None would maintain that their leaders hoped for immediate success at the polls. At best, they could do no more than to organize a small group of disciplined party workers who would continuously propagandize for the solution of economic ills along lines of nationalization. These evangelists of future

THE MINOR PARTY MISSION

property dispensation labored in a hostile world, a world in which tariffs, subsidies, wages and hour legislation, regulation of corporations, and a multitude of other contemporary capitalist problems furnished subjects for political discussion.

It is impossible to evaluate the influence of minor parties in their effect upon the public thinking. Yet none will deny that the Liberty and Free Soil parties did much to crystallize northern opinion upon the slavery issue before the Civil War. The agrarian protest movement was largely instrumental in the creation of the Interstate Commerce Commission. The Greenbackers, the Populists, and the Socialists did valiant service in the education of the American public for the regulation of public utilities and the addition of the income-tax amendment. And the Populists were largely responsible for the adoption of the initiative, the referendum, and the recall provisions of many state constitutions. The list of these contributions to American institutions might be expanded over many pages, but the above are sufficient to illustrate the minor-party rôle in the popularization of ideas to the point at which the realistic major parties can, without alienation of public support, include them in their official programs. It is almost a biological law of American politics that, when a minor party succeeds, it dies. It must submit to being devoured!

Despite popular misconception, minor parties have also on many occasions, by drawing support from one or the other of the major parties, determined the winner of a presidential contest. The election of 1844 was won by James K. Polk, but if the Liberty party had not polled 15,000 votes in New York, largely at the expense of the Whigs, Henry Clay would certainly have been elected president of the United States.

133

He might then have been both "right" and "President." Polk's New York's plurality was only slightly over five thousand votes. Thus while Birney's Liberty party poll was only sixty-two thousand for the entire United States, he polled enough votes in the most vital state—New York—to determine the national party winner.

As has been seen, most minor parties are sectional in popularity. The national vote percentages are therefore of little importance in evaluating the effect of their votes upon the outcome of national elections. In 1884, Benjamin Butler's New York Greenback poll of 16,994 gave that state and the national election to Grover Cleveland and the Democrats. Four years later, the Prohibition vote of that state, if it had been given to Cleveland, would have resulted in his re-election to the presidency.

In 1892, the popular pluralities which Cleveland received in California, Delaware, Illinois, Indiana, Missouri, New York, North Carolina, West Virginia, and Wisconsin were sufficient to give him 277 electoral votes to 145 for Harrison. Yet, if Harrison had won these plurality elections—and without Populist and Prohibition opposition he might have won all except Delaware, North Carolina, and West Virginia—he would easily have won in the electoral college. In 1916, the Prohibitionists alone polled enough votes in California and Connecticut to give the electoral votes of those states to President Wilson, though in both cases the Socialists could, by supporting Wilson, have elected him over a Republican-Prohibition coalition.

Upon the general influence of minor parties, Professor John D. Hicks writes: "Far more depressing to the ordinary elector, however, would be the discovery that the United States has never possessed for any considerable period of time the two party system in its pure and undefiled form. It is a fact, easily demonstrated, that at least for the last hundred years one formidable third party has succeeded another with bewildering rapidity; and that, contrary to the customary view, these third parties have seriously affected the results of presidential elections, have frequently had a hand in the determination of important national policies, and have played perhaps quite as important a rôle as either of the major parties in making the nation what it is to-day."[20]

[20] "The Third Party Tradition in American Politics," *The Mississippi Valley Historical Review*, XX, No. 1, (June, 1933), 3-28.

★ ★ ★ ★ ★

CHAPTER FOUR

The Electoral College

★ ★ ★ ★ ★ ★ ★ ★

THOUGH important as an index of political thinking, popular-vote totals do not in themselves determine the outcome of national elections. Triumph depends upon the operation of the electoral college. A political party may well win an election over a larger party, depending upon the distribution of votes in what have come to be known as "key" states. It has only to be remembered that in 1884 Cleveland won the thirty-five electoral votes of New York with a plurality of only 1,149 popular votes—an average of less than thirty-three voters for each electoral vote! The plurality in this election constituted but nine-hundredths of one per cent of the total New York vote.

Again, in 1892, the Republicans carried Ohio and twenty-two of its twenty-three electoral votes with a plurality of only 1,072 popular votes. The total Ohio vote in this election was 850,166 and the Republican plurality was but one-tenth of one per cent of the total. In 1916, the twelve electoral votes of Minnesota went with a 392 Republican plurality, which was only one-tenth of one per cent of the total Minnesota poll. Thus in these three contests selected for illustration, the average plurality, per electoral vote, was less than thirty-eight votes. Such illustrations are not, of course, common occurrences in American political history, but they depict nevertheless the potential injustice of such a system. Candidates of lesser parties have been elected even though they received fewer popular votes than their unsuccessful rivals. The elections of 1876 and 1888 were of this character. In the former year, Samuel Tilden, Democrat, received 264,-202 more votes than the victorious Hayes;[1] and in 1888 Grover Cleveland, Democratic candidate for re-election, out-polled the triumphant Harrison by 100,476 votes.

In contests such as those in 1880, 1884, 1888, 1892, 1912, and 1916, third parties secured enough votes to prevent either of the larger parties from receiving an absolute popular majority. As has been noted in the preceding discussion, these minor parties affected the popular vote of first one and then of the other. The Democrats lost most heavily in 1892 in popular vote, the Republicans in 1912, and the Democrats again in 1924. There exists no formula to determine which party will suffer through minor-party competition.

In *Figure 5*, the party aspects of the electoral college are shown for the nineteen elections. Thirteen of the elections went to the Republicans. Curiously enough, all but two of these occur in clusters—five from 1864 to 1880, four from 1896 to 1908, and three from 1920 to 1928. The Democrats were discredited during and immediately following the Civil War. The union of the Democrats with the "radical" Populists likewise caused the party to lose political respect and left the Republicans in almost unopposed operation of the national government. With the passing of the Democratic alternative in the years after the turn of the century, the preponder-

[1] These figures are from the official Democratic count.

ant party could well afford the luxury of intra-party dissension. It was to rue its indulgence in 1912. In that year, polling fewer popular votes than Bryan did in 1908, Woodrow Wilson captured the largest electoral-college total until Herbert Hoover swamped Governor Smith in 1928.

Though returned to power by the narrowest of margins in 1916, the Democrats thereafter fell to their lowest estate since the early Reconstruction days. Speculation was rife

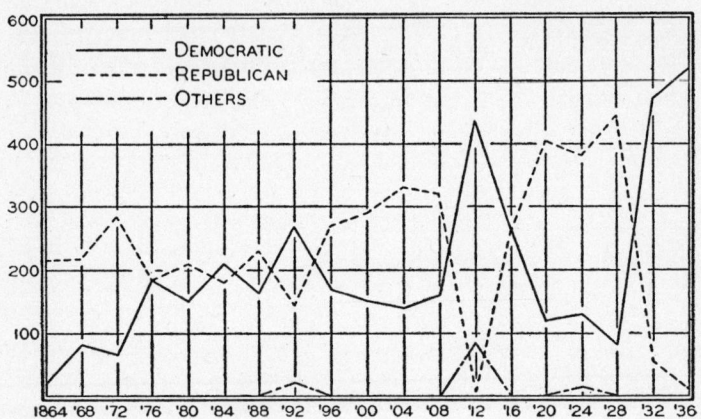

Figure 5.—Electoral College Votes: by Parties

whether the party of Jackson and Cleveland would ever recapture the favor of the voters. The Republicans furnished the answer by clinging too closely to the program of "big business"; and the common man, in a new display of traditional militancy, smote the Republicans with a ferocity not experienced by the party since the Civil War. The 1912 defeat was not analogous, for then the recalcitrant Republicans voted for a Republican and not for the Democratic candidate. The Progressives regarded Theodore Roosevelt as a "real" Republican. In 1920 and 1924, the Democrats were saved by sectionalism. In the periods of unpopularity, the Democrats could rely upon the unswerving devotion of the South. The Republicans have no such section from which they can rally their forces for an appeal to the rest of the country.

After viewing the graph (*Figure 5*) in its entirety, one thing becomes apparent. The period of close rivalry between the Republicans and Democrats was terminated with the election of 1896. A new era was born in that campaign, an era which has been characterized by landslide elections and the turning from office of a party by a preponderance similar to that by which it came to power. In other words, the voters of the country have cast overboard the traditional party loyalties. The allegiances of agrarian democracy retreated before the new industrial order in the United States.

The most devastating criticism of the electoral college system concerns the complete loss of minority votes in a state. A bare plurality is sufficient to win the entire electoral vote of a state. Many public figures, headed by Senator Norris, are repeating the customary appeals to fairness and equity. They maintain, and with reason, that this unique system of representative democracy violates fundamental ethical criteria. The whole doctrine of proportional representation arises from this same political and ethical feeling. The plight of the Republicans in the seven middle western states in 1932 illustrates this inequity in the operation of the electoral college. In that election, President Hoover received 5,440,493 votes in the Middle West. These consti-

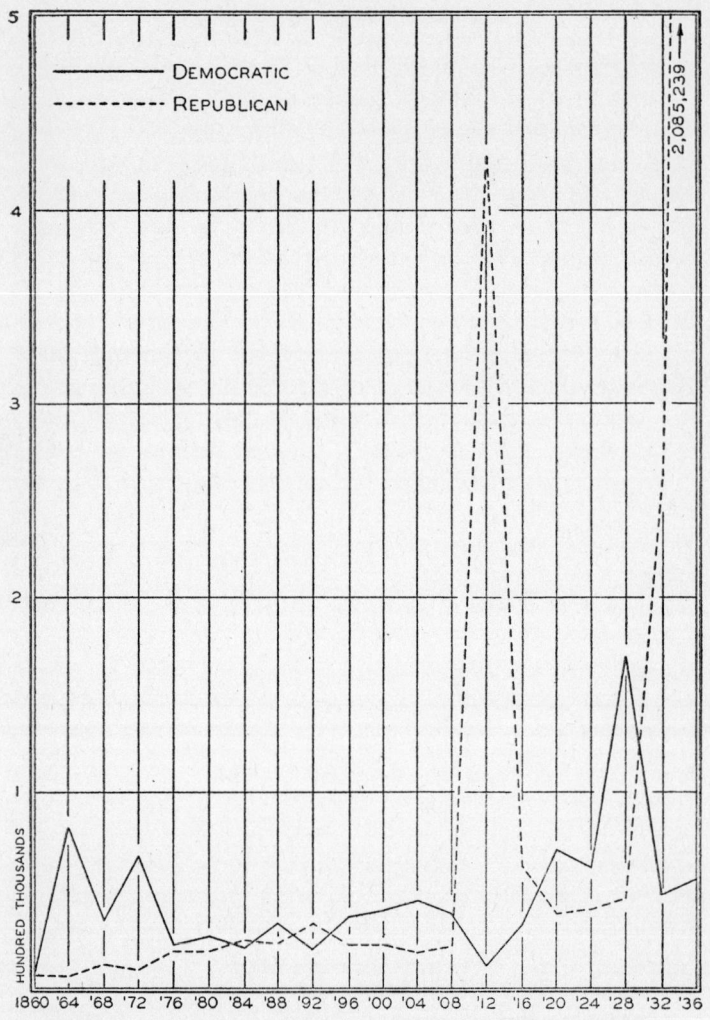

Figure 6.—Popular Votes per Electoral Vote: by Parties

tuted 43.83 per cent of its total poll. For these more than five million votes, the Republicans received not one electoral vote. On the other hand, the Democrats, with only 6,587,141 votes, having pluralities in every state, took every one of the 122 electoral votes. Thus, the Democrats received an electoral vote for only 53,993 popular votes. On the other hand, if the Republicans had secured electoral votes according to the same yardstick, they would have had 101 to 122 for the Democrats. In the same election, the Democrats received 177 electoral votes in the South and Border states with a popular vote total of but 5,947,785. Under such conditions, the result was such as practically to give electoral-college votes to very small pluralities. Though polling but half-a-million more votes in the South and Border than the Republicans received in the Middle West, the Democrats received 177 electoral votes, or one electoral vote for 2,866 plurality ballots.

The popular-vote factor in the electoral college from 1860 to 1936 is shown in *Figure 6*. It is an interesting graph, for behind it lies an undeniable interpretation of American politics of the past eighty years. Tagged with the label of rebellion during the Civil War, the Democrats did not rise to a position of respectability until 1876. In the three elections (1864, 1868, and 1872), the Republicans received 712 electoral votes to 167 for the Democrats. Thus Lincoln and Grant took 81 per cent of the electoral vote with but 54.39 per cent of the popular vote. In other words, in these three elections, an electoral vote cost the Republicans but 12,383 popular votes. Simultaneously, an electoral vote cost the Democrats 44,073 votes. Consequently, the price which the Democrats paid for the South's being heavily allied with their party was that of receiving but 19 per cent of the electoral vote with 45.4 per cent of the popular vote.

The period of most equitable operation was that from 1876 to 1896. In those six elections, four of which were won by the Republicans, the disparity in party quotients was the smallest for the entire period. In each election, the quotient of the triumphant party was, of course, smaller than that of the loser. In the five elections (1876-1892), the Republicans were out-polled both in popular and electoral college votes. Their average for the 961 electoral votes which they received was 25,984 popular votes. On the other hand, the Democrats gave but 24,471 votes each for their electoral votes. Third parties were the big losers in this period, polling 2,275,636 popular votes and receiving but twenty-one electoral votes,[2] for a quotient of 108,364 popular votes.

The four elections from 1896 to 1908 saw the Republicans victorious, with electoral-vote quotients that were reminiscent of the Reconstruction period. The largest disparity since 1872 was achieved in 1904, when the Democratic quotient of 36,339 was 60 per cent in excess of the Republicans' 22,705. Bryan's 1908 quotient of 39,555 was 65.38 per cent above the Republicans' mark.

Since 1912, the electoral-college quotients of the two parties have shifted to extremes. Party allegiances began to crumble in 1896, but the last seven elections have produced unanswerable evidence of that political disintegration. The quotients varied from the 14,442 of the Democrats in 1912 to the 2,083,648 of the Republicans in 1936. The latter is,

---

[2] For Weaver in 1892. Actually, in that election the party quotas were: Democratic, 22,060; Republican, 35,693; and Populist, 62,115. The popular votes of the Prohibitionists and Socialist-Laborites were completely wasted.

of course, a practical *ne plus ultra*. These figures prove, better than the most consummate rhetoric, the indisputable vagaries of the electoral-college system. Incidentally, this 1912 quotient of the Democrats was the lowest for the period from 1876 to 1936.[3] It derived in the vigorous clash of the two factions of the 1912 Republican party.

The closest approximation to proportional representation in the electoral college came in 1916, when the Republican quotient was but 1.98 per cent above that of the Democrats. The point farthest from this ideal occurred in 1936 when the Republican figure was 3,827.19 per cent above that of the Democrats. The highest Democratic quotient of the seventy-six years was 172,603 in 1928, while the Republicans three times exceeded that mark—1912, 1932, and 1936.

From 1864 to 1936, a total of 8,428 electoral votes were cast, of which 4,446 (52.75 per cent) were Republican, 3,860 (45.80 per cent) were Democratic, and 122 (1.45 per cent) were for third parties. If the last two Democratic landslides are omitted from these totals, and if only the records of the seventeen elections (1864-1928), are considered, the party percentages of electoral votes are: Republican, 59.64; Democratic, 38.69; and third parties, 1.66.

Prior to 1932, the Democrats persistently criticized the electoral-college system because it militated on many occasions against the chances for Democratic victory. In TABLE 13, the party deviations from the absolutely equitable electoral-college quotients, derived from division of the total popular vote by total electoral vote, are shown for each of the nineteen elections.

[3] The Republican quotients of 1864, 1868, and 1872 were, respectively, 10,993, 14,079, and 12,577.

PRESIDENTIAL ELECTIONS

In the seventy-two-year period, the Republicans have been distinctly favored in the operation of the electoral college. With 48.07 per cent of the popular vote they have won 52.75 per cent of the electoral votes, while the Democrats

TABLE 13.—PARTY PERCENTAGE DEVIATIONS FROM ABSOLUTE ELECTORAL COLLEGE QUOTIENTS OF NATIONAL POPULAR VOTE

Year	Absolute Quotient	Republican + or −	Democratic + or −	Minor + or −	Republican or Democratic excess over other
1864	17,231	− 36.20	+ 407.39		D. 695.31
1868	19,468	− 27.68	+ 73.57		D. 140.01
1872	18,385	− 31.59	+134.06		D. 242.15
1876	22,778	− 4.33	+ 2.61		D. 7.26
1880	24,937	− 16.63	+ 14.92		D. 37.84
1884	26,192	+ 1.78	− 15.01		R. 19.76
1888	28,355	− 17.66	+ 16.30		D. 41.25
1892	27,153	+ 31.20	− 26.12	+128.75	R. 77.59
1896	30,805	− 14.81	+ 20.06		D. 40.93
1900	31,049	− 20.37	+ 32.13		D. 65.93
1904	28,096	− 19.19	+ 29.26		D. 59.95
1908	30,528	− 21.65	+ 29.57		D. 65.38
1912	28,307	+1438.91	− 48.98	+111.20	R. 2916.33
1916	34,514	− 2.69	− 4.73		R. 1.98
1920	50,257	− 20.45	+ 42.45		D. 79.07
1924	54,750	− 24.69	+ 17.65	+596.95	D. 56.24
1928	69,318	− 30.49	+149.00		D. 266.54
1932	74,818	+ 257.07	− 35.37		R. 452.52
1936	85,504	+2336.90	− 61.16		R. 3827.19
1864-36	39,572	− 8.87	+ 0.95	+292.07	D. 10.78

have received but 45.80 per cent of the electoral votes with 46.25 per cent of the popular ballots. Minor parties were even more roughly handled. With 5.67 per cent of the popular vote, they got but 1.45 per cent of the electoral count. In this period the average Republican electoral quotient was 8.87

THE ELECTORAL COLLEGE

per cent smaller than the absolutely equitable standard, while that of the Democrats was 0.95 per cent larger. For the nineteen elections, the Democratic quotient was 10.78 per cent larger than that of their more successful rivals.

In fourteen of the nineteen elections, the Republican quotient was less than the proportional one,[4] while the Democrats were thus favored in but six.[5] Both were under the authentic standard in 1916, which, next to 1876, shows the fairest operation of the system. The distribution of party strength in these contests was such as to give each party its just electoral-college count. That, however, was merely an accident, for the results on a national scale only happened to approximate the ideal. It was achieved as the result of many downright inequities in individual states.[6] The statistical averages appear much better than the data from which the averages are drawn.

The Sections in the Electoral College

As has been observed, the East has been a dominant Republican section; this generalization applies more aptly to the six New England states. Of these six states from 1864 to 1892, only Connecticut presents a record of Democratic success. In the eight elections Connecticut went Democratic

[4] The Republicans won all of these elections except that of 1916.
[5] The Democrats won all of these national elections (1884, 1892, 1912, 1916, 1932, and 1936).
[6] For instance, in 1916, in sixteen states the plurality of popular votes for the election was less than 5 per cent. Thus, a shift of any dimensions over 2½ per cent would have changed the outcome in those sixteen states. Of these sixteen the Republicans took Maine, Massachusetts, Connecticut, Delaware, West Virginia, South Dakota, Indiana, Minnesota, and Oregon. The Democrats carried Missouri, Kansas, North Dakota, New Hampshire, New Mexico, California, and Washington.

in four. Thus, for this sectional subdivision, the Republicans were victorious in 91.33 per cent of the forty-eight state contests. Since 1892, the Democrats have enjoyed slightly greater success, winning in fourteen of sixty-six contests. Massachusetts and Rhode Island, most Democratic of the six, have each returned the party victorious in four elections.[7] Yet in seven of the eleven elections, the Republicans have swept the entire electoral vote. The Democrats won five state contests in 1912, one in 1916, two in 1928, two in 1932, and four in 1936. Thus, until 1932, the six states had gone to the Republicans in eighty-eight of the 102 contests. In total electoral votes for the entire period, 629 of the 774, or 81.3 per cent, were Republican. If one omits the elections of 1912, 1932, and 1936—all national Democratic triumphs in the electoral college—the New England Republican total of 597 completely overpowers the Democratic fifty-one. During the period, Vermont did not cast one Democratic electoral vote; Maine, New Hampshire, Massachusetts, and Rhode Island were exclusively Republican ground from 1864 to 1908. In the ten elections from 1896 to 1932, Connecticut went Democratic only in 1912.

The North Atlantic states of the East present a different general political picture. Pennsylvania became synonymous with Republicanism, a label which the state merited. In the nineteen elections, the Democrats were victors in only one—the last (1936)—though the Progressives took the electoral vote in 1912 from their "Stand-pat" Republican rivals. On the other hand, New Jersey, like Connecticut, did not become a Republican province until after the infusion of the interventionist Populist views into the Democratic body.

[7] 1912, 1928, 1932, and 1936.

THE ELECTORAL COLLEGE

From 1896 to 1932, the Democrats won only the election of 1912. Thus, New Jersey was as regular as Pennsylvania, except that she gave Wilson, her not-too-popular "native-son," a twenty-five thousand plurality over "T. R." in 1912. Incidentally, this 1912 plurality amounted to but 5.91 per cent of the total popular vote. And Wilson's total was but 40.5 per cent of the state poll. On the other hand, from 1864 to 1892, the Democrats had won seven of the eight New Jersey contests, losing only in 1872.

New York is the key state of the section. Her electoral vote has practically equaled the combined total of the six New England states. From 1864 to 1892, she gave 139 electoral votes to the Republicans and 140 to the Democrats. Reflecting the sentiment of her section, after the Democratic fusion she returned the Republicans victorious in eight of the next nine elections, straying only in 1912. Her Democratic preference in the last two elections needs no comment. Of her 748 total electoral poll since the Civil War, 469, or 62.7 per cent, have gone to the Republicans.

Since the Civil War, then, the East has been a real bulwark for the Republicans. Only in 1912, 1932, and 1936, did the Democrats carry the section. This Republican dominance represents 74.43 per cent of the total electoral vote, as against 33.96 per cent for the Democrats, and 1.60 per cent for the Bull-Moose Progressives.

The five Border states have been strong, but not exclusive, Democratic territory. Before 1896, the *ante bellum* traditions kept the votes generally in support of the Democratic party while the Republicans were able to win only 13.44 per cent of the electoral poll. But after the Populist amalgamation the section altered its political habits sufficiently to give the

Republicans 47.93 per cent of the electoral vote. Kentucky and Missouri were the most Democratic during this latter period. For the nineteen elections, the Democrats took 64.3 per cent of the total electoral count, leaving the Republicans with 35.7 per cent. No Border elector has ever cast his vote for a third party candidate.

The South has been almost exclusively a one-party section, more so than any other. Of the 2,072 total electoral votes, the Democrats have taken 1,871, or 90.35 per cent. Of the 201 Republican electoral votes, 107 were cast during Reconstruction days (1868-1876). Thus, from 1880 to 1936, the Democrats have taken 94.9 per cent of the southern electoral total. They executed a "grand slam" from 1880 to 1916. In 1920, Oklahoma and Tennessee broke with the sectional tradition. And in 1928, the anti-Smith feeling took Virginia, North Carolina, Tennessee, Florida, Texas, and Oklahoma into the Republican column. Throughout the seventy-two-year period, Georgia has never elected a Republican elector, even though, in 1928, she narrowly missed that distinction.

The Middle West has since 1864 been the dominant Republican section. Of its 2,060 electoral total, that party has received 1,571, or 76.26 per cent. The Democrats, always strong in the section, received 21.79 per cent, and minor parties but 1.94 per cent. In the first eight elections, the Republicans took 88.54 per cent of the electoral count, even though the Democrats polled over 45 per cent of the popular vote. The Democrats carried the section in 1892, 1912, 1932, and 1936. The Republicans were completely blanked in the last three of those Democratic years, a fact which reveals how solidly the section votes. In only five of the nineteen elections has there been division of votes among the

THE ELECTORAL COLLEGE

section's electoral-college delegations. From 1864 to 1928, the section gave the Republicans 86.51 per cent, the Democrats 11.28 per cent, and the third parties 2.2 per cent of the total electoral vote.

The West has given the Republicans a bare majority in the electoral college—614 of the 1,060 votes. Against this 57.92 per cent share, the Democrats have secured 402 (37.92 per cent) and the minor parties 44 (4.15 per cent). The Republicans carried every election from 1864 to 1888 and took 92.52 per cent of the electors. Beginning in 1892, the Democrats and minor parties have held the Republicans to a 51.77 per cent share, polling 435 to the Republicans' 467 electoral votes.

To summarize the discussion on this point, little remains except the tabulation of the party distribution of electoral votes. These are shown by sections in TABLE 14. The Middle West and the East have been the dominant Republican sections and, because of their enormous populations, have furnished the sinews of Republican victory. The South has been religiously Democratic, except in the Reconstruction period. Since 1892, the Border has become a strong battleground for the two parties. The West reversed its early Republican predilections and, since the fusionist period, has given the Republicans only a slight edge over the Democrats and the minor parties. From 1896 to 1928, the East, Middle West and Border alliance, with some assistance from the West, guaranteed Republican success whenever the party presented a unified leadership. The break in 1932 was too general a political phenomenon to be explained from the standpoint of geography.

The Clash of Parties

It is axiomatic to remark that pluralities, not total votes on a national basis, select American presidents and vice-presidents. The American presidential election is not, strictly speaking, a national election. It is a combination of forty-eight state contests. Thus, as happened in 1888, a party

TABLE 14.—SECTIONAL ASPECTS OF THE ELECTORAL COLLEGE VOTE, 1864-1936

Section	1864 - 1936					
	Republican		Democratic		Others	
	Vote	%	Vote	%	Vote	%
East	1758	74.43	566	23.95	38	1.61
Border	302	34.56	572	65.44		
South	201	9.70	1871	90.30		
M. W.	1571	74.91	449	22.11	40	1.97
West	614	57.92	402	37.92	44	4.15
U. S.	4446	52.75	3860	45.79	122	1.45

may lose an election even though it receives a plurality in the popular vote. The Democrats lost this contest because their votes were not properly distributed. They carried many states by huge majorities—and lost too many by small pluralities. It is well to bear this point in mind while looking at the clash of parties in the various sections.

Since 1864, 161 of the 812 contests in states have been won by no more than a 5 per cent plurality. Sixteen of these were in 1916, thirteen in 1888, twelve in 1892, eleven in 1876, and ten in 1884. Of the eleven elections after 1892, only those of 1912 and 1916 equal the average of 9.25 per cent established from 1864 to 1896—an average created with fewer states participating in the elections. As a matter of fact, up to 1892 one state of every four (25.08 per cent) decided the contest over party electors by less than a 5 per cent plurality. After 1892, only one state in ten (10.64 per cent) has presented such close contests. This demonstrates again the bandwagon tendencies of the electorate after 1896. Even when the opposition overthrew the government, the margin was decisive in the latter period. Party members refused to maintain their allegiances. The maturing industrial order created a feeling of economic insecurity in many of those engaged in it and an antipathy in many not so vitally affected. This skepticism and uneasiness were transferred to the political arena when campaign programs were formulated. In TABLE 15 the 5 per cent elections are shown by years and sections. The perceptible break in the close-election tradition is shown in the percentage category. Nine of the last eleven elections (1896-1936) were below the general average as against two out of the eight in the preceding period.

Five Per Cent Plurality Elections in the Separate Sections

Having 29.95 per cent of the individual elections, the East had 30.4 per cent of the 5 per cent contests. With eleven of her nineteen elections within the category, Connecticut led the section. New Hampshire was second with nine; New York had eight, and New Jersey seven. On the other hand, Vermont had but one (1912), Maine two (1912 and 1916), Rhode Island three, and Massachusetts and Pennsylvania four each. Interestingly enough, of the forty-nine

TABLE 15.—FIVE-PER-CENT PLURALITY ELECTIONS BY YEARS AND SECTIONS

	East	Border	South	M. W.	West	U. S.	% States
1864	3	1				4	16.0
1868	4	1	1	2	2	10	27.7†
1872	1	3	3			7	18.9
1876	4		3	4	2	13	35.1‡
1880	5	1	1	2	3	12	31.6
1884	4	1	1	4		10	26.3
1888	4	3	2	4	1	14	36.8
1892	5	2		5	5	17	38.6
1896		1		2	5	8	17.8
1900		1		1	3	5	11.1
1904		3				3	6.7
1908		3		1	4	8	17.4
1912	7			1	8	16	33.3
1916	4	3		2	7	16	33.3
1920		1	1			2	4.2
1924		2	1		1	4	8.3
1928	3		2			5	10.4
1932	4	1		1		6	12.5
1936	1					1	2.1
Total	49	27	15	29	41*	161*	19.8
Won by Republicans	25	10	7	22	14	78	9.6
Won by Democrats	24	17	8	7	26	82	10.2

* One won by Populist (1892).

† Florida electors appointed by legislature.

‡ Colorado electors appointed by legislature.

contests, the Republicans won twenty-five and the Democrats twenty-four. The Republicans profited especially in Pennsylvania where all four were won by them and in New Hampshire where they won six of the nine. The Democrats took six of the seven in New Jersey, three of the four in Massachusetts, two of the three in Rhode Island, four of the eight in New York, and five of the eleven in Connecticut.

The temporal distribution of these eastern contests is an interesting phenomenon. Until the Populist-Democratic fusion, Connecticut was exclusively in this close bracket. Of these eight elections, (1864-1892), each of the two major parties won four. After 1896, the state was fairly safe Republican ground. New Jersey traveled the same route politically. New York had seven 5 per cent contests before 1896, with 1872, the year of Grant's re-election, the only exception. Four of the first five Pennsylvania contests were 5 per cent ones, but thereafter (1880), the Republicans assumed the upper hand until 1936. In New Hampshire five of the first eight were within this classification. Seven of the nine states had 5 per cent contests in 1912, and four in 1916. The Democrats won six of the 1912 contests,[8] but only one in 1916 (New Hampshire). Governor Smith's popularity brought New York, Massachusetts, and Rhode Island within the category in 1928; of the three he lost only his home state.

The Border states had twenty-seven (28.4 per cent) elections within the 5 per cent category. Delaware had seven, West Virginia and Kentucky six each, and Maryland and Missouri four each. The Democrats profited greatly in that

---

[8] Maine, New Hampshire, Massachusetts, Rhode Island, Connecticut, and New Jersey. Vermont was Republican. New York and Pennsylvania were outside the bracket.

they won seventeen. Before 1916, the Republicans had won but five of twenty such contests, but thereafter they lost only two of the seven. Before 1896, the Democrats won ten of twelve. From 1872 to 1916, twenty-one of the sixty contests were within the category, and the Democrats won all but seven. Six of the eight Kentucky elections from 1896 to 1924 were 5 per cent contests and the Democrats won four of them. The others were scattered with no more than three coming in succession in any state.[9] Three of the five states, though not the same states each time, had similar close contests in 1872, 1888, 1904, 1908, and 1916. These were the years in which the Border Democrats were seriously challenged by the Republicans, but the latter won only six of the fifteen contests.

The South, a one-party section, would naturally have fewer 5 per cent elections than the other sections. Only fifteen of the 202 contests were within the scope of this classification and eleven of these came from 1868 to 1888. From 1892 to 1916, the Democrats encountered no such opposition in any of the twelve states. Since 1920, there have been four—Tennessee (1920), Oklahoma (1924), and Alabama and Texas (1928). Of the fifteen contests, the Republicans won eight, though two of those went to them by virtue of the questionable decision of the Electoral Commission of 1877.

The Middle West has been a real battleground for the major parties, and especially does this apply to those five states east of the Mississippi. Twenty-nine of the 133 middle western elections (21.8 per cent) were within the classification. Indiana is the real leader with ten out of nineteen, but Ohio had seven, Illinois four, and Michigan and

[9] Delaware, 1864, 1868, 1872; and West Virginia, 1884, 1888, and 1892.

THE ELECTORAL COLLEGE

Wisconsin three each. Minnesota and Iowa were low with one each. The most important part of these close clashes was the winning percentage of the Republicans. This party won twenty-two of the twenty-nine contests (75.9 per cent). In Michigan, the Republicans won three out of three, in Ohio six out of seven, in Illinois three out of four, in Wisconsin two out of three, and in Indiana seven out of ten.

The section was much more bitterly contested before the Populist fusion. From 1864 to 1892, twenty-one of the forty elections were 5 per cent ones. There were six in Indiana, five in Ohio, four in Illinois, and three each in Michigan and Wisconsin. After 1892 there was none in Michigan, Illinois, or Wisconsin, but one each in Minnesota and Iowa, and two in Ohio. Since 1920 there has been but one (Ohio, 1932). This section best illustrates the large scale changes in political allegiance.

Though the section of largest minor-party support, the West is, except for the South, the lowest in percentage of close elections. Only forty-one of its 207 contests (19.8 per cent) are within this class. Curiously enough, this was also the percentage mark for the entire United States, which means that the South pulled the national average down to the West's figure, for the East, Border, and Middle West were all above the national average.

The surprisingly low figure of the West needs some explanation. For instance, 157 of the section's 207 elections (75.8 per cent) came after the fusion of Populists and Democrats, or in the period of stampeding majorities. Before 1896 the national ratio was 29.5 per cent; from that time it fell to 14.3 per cent for these close contests. The change in the political temper of the United States is revealed by these significant figures. Thus, in the light of these observations, the West's record is obviously one of relatively close political struggle. In fact, since 1896, it has exceeded the national average in the percentage of close elections—17.8 per cent as against the combined sectional average of 14.3 per cent. In this matter, the West's percentage mark was exceeded only by the Border's 27.3 per cent and the East's 20.2 per cent. The Middle West had 9.1 per cent and the South a lowly 3.1 per cent.

California, with seven 5 per cent contests, and Oregon with six, lead the West. Kansas and North Dakota had four each, and Nebraska, Colorado, Wyoming, and Nevada three each. Montana, New Mexico, Arizona, and Washington have had but one each. Those with two were Idaho, Utah, and South Dakota. The Democrats have emerged far ahead of the Republicans in the clash. However, in the three Pacific states, the Republicans took eight of fourteen contests. In the twelve plains' and mountain states, the Democrats captured seventeen out of twenty-seven.

The temporal distribution of the West's close elections is interesting. There were eight in 1912, seven in 1916, five each in 1892 and 1896, four in 1908, and three each in 1880 and 1900. The Democrats won seven of the eight in 1912, five out of seven in 1916, and three out of five in 1896. Thus in these three elections, this party received fifteen of its total twenty-three victories.

Ten Per Cent Plurality Elections

The establishment of criteria for determining the effectiveness of a political party system is difficult at best. Disregarding the factors that operate to prevent the free orientation of citizens into parties according to agreement with avowed party policies, an opposition party ought to have the respect, if not the allegiance, of a great majority of ctziens. Under these conditions, the abandonment of the party in power by large numbers of its former supporters would return this respectable opposition to power in the next election. Such a condition, revealing periodic changes of party, contributes to the internal strength of a great national state. The leaders of no party should succeed when they openly flout the best judgment of the citizenry. And if that leadership is faced with the probability of being reduced to the rôle of the opposition after the next election, the use of high office for mere personal or party ends is less likely to occur.

There is another point that ought to be mentioned. If party programs are maintained at a standard close to the wishes of the electorate, the threat of violence is substantially reduced. Change, under these circumstances, is gradual but fairly consistent. It is only when a successful party, generally by indirection and subterfuge, disregards the welfare of great groups of people that direct action enters the political scene. There are many who deprecate the economic aspects of political alignment in America, but these people are for the most part cowering before an abstract formula. Can a political party system function without this economic differentiation? It must be remembered that the public welfare is not some vaulted refuge to which the spirits of men fly to escape the continuous ills of this mundane existence. On the contrary, it is omnipresent and earthy. It is the mechanism of a happy and prosperous people and is in nowise alien to bread, potatoes, houses, shoes, and mortgages.

PRESIDENTIAL ELECTIONS

To take these practical features from political party struggle is simply to deny the *raison d'etre* of a party system and of democracy. Democracy emerged as a social instrument for protection against the realistic practices of political tyranny. As it matured, and after the threat of such arbitrariness became no more than a historical phenomenon, men's thinking turned to the economic aspects of the good life. And the latter will not be erased unless these political liberties are again jeopardized.

If all states had had elections of only 5 per cent pluralities, there could be little criticism of the American party system. The record of 20 per cent for the close elections is meritorious, but it might have been better, both in the Reconstruction period and in the period since 1920. Again, party balance is maintained through sectional points of view—one of this country's principal weaknesses And party leaders are not always astute in interpreting the inarticulate hopes and aspirations of the common people. That is an inherent weakness in all collective enterprise. With these two prevailing impediments to any party system, Americans may well be amazed at the fact that 20 per cent of their contests in states have been decided upon so narrow a margin as 5 per cent. In order to prevent the free play necessary to education of both the leaders and the ordinary members of political parties, so close a division should not be expected. Even a 10 per cent plurality gives to the opposition an opportunity to come to power if the government makes an error of serious consequence.

From 1864 to 1936, there were 268 (33.2 per cent of the total) contests of the 10 per cent character. Of these, the Republicans won 146 (54.5 per cent), the Democrats 119

THE ELECTORAL COLLEGE

(44.4 per cent), and minor parties three (1.1 per cent). The success of the Republicans here is in strange contrast to their record in the 5 per cent elections. In that contrast lies much of the secret of their domination of public affairs during the seventy-two-year period.

The sectional averages follow the trends of the 5 per cent contests. In the five Border states, 45.5 per cent of all contests were within the 10 per cent classification, while the East's mark was 40.3 per cent, the Middle West's 39 per cent, the West's 30.1 per cent, and the South's, a poor last, 19 per cent. The South and West were below the national average, and the other three sections well above it. One hundred and thirty-seven came before 1896, and 131 thereafter. Thus, 47.2 per cent of the earlier elections were within the 10 per cent range, but the mark of the modern period was only 25.8 per cent. This reveals the profound shift in politics after the turn of the century. The shift is even more pronounced when it is pointed out that forty-six of these 131 recent contests occurred in 1912 and 1916, years of Republican squabbling. The remaining eighty-five contests are divided among the other nine elections, leaving an average of 20.7 per cent. In the five elections since 1920, the mark is 16.6 per cent. Between 1880 and 1892, it was 51.3 per cent. The elections in which at least one-half of the state contests were within the 10 per cent plurality range were 1884, 1888, 1892, and 1916; those of from 40 per cent to 50 per cent were 1872, 1876, 1880, and 1912; between 30 per cent and 40 per cent, 1864, 1868, and 1900; between 20 per cent and 30 per cent, 1896, 1908, 1924, 1928, and 1932; and those under 20 per cent, 1904, 1920, and 1936. Thus eight of the last eleven elections are in the

PRESIDENTIAL ELECTIONS

two lowest brackets, in which there was no representative before 1896.

Connecticut, New Hampshire, Ohio, and Indiana have each had twelve of their nineteen elections within the 10 per cent class; New York has had eleven, and New Jersey, Delaware, Maryland, and West Virginia ten each. Those with nine were Kentucky, Tennessee, and Oregon; those with eight, Massachusetts, Pennsylvania, Missouri, North Carolina, Illinois, Wisconsin, Kansas, and California. On the

TABLE 16.—PARTY WINNERS OF 10 PER CENT ELECTIONS BY SECTIONS AND PERIODS

(R., Republican; D., Democrat; M., Minor Parties)

	1864-76		1880-1892			1896-1916			1920-36		1864-1936		
	R.	D.	R.	D.	M.	R.	D.	M.	R.	D.	R.	D.	M.
East	13	6	16	9		7	6	1	5	6	41	27	1
Border	2	3		13		11	10		5	3	18	29	
South	10	3		9			7		6	3	16	22	
M. W.	12	1	15	4		11	5		2	2	40	12	
West	5	1	10	3	2	10	23		6	2	31	29	2
United States	42	14	41	38	2	39	51	1	24	16	146	119	3

other hand, Mississippi has had none; and Vermont, South Carolina, Georgia, and Louisiana have had one such contest each.

The sectional distribution of party winners, as shown in TABLE 16, is interesting. The contribution of the Middle West to Republican success has long been emphasized, but the figures in the table make that observation indisputable. In almost 77 per cent of this section's 10 per cent contests, the Republicans eked out victories in the electoral college. In 1888, the Republicans won all six 10 per cent contests in the section, in 1916 five out of six, in 1884 and 1876 four out of five. The only profitable years for the Democrats were 1912, with three out of three, and 1892 with three out of six contests. Thus one-half of the Democratic triumphs were in those two elections.

The East returned the Republicans victorious in almost 60 per cent of the close contests, but only in 1912 and 1916 were there party sweeps of a large number of contests. In the former year, the Democrats took five out of seven, but the Republicans came back four years later to take five out of six. These 1916 results were a duplication of 1880. However, the Republicans took four out of four contests in 1872, and four out of six in 1888. Besides 1912, the best Democratic years were 1876, with three out of five and 1892, with three out of six.

In this clash between parties, the West showed little preference. The best Republican years were 1892, with seven out of eight contests, and 1924 with five out of five. The Democrats took four out of six in 1896, three out of five in 1908, ten of the eleven in 1912 and five of the seven in 1916. Thus, in these four elections the Democrats received twenty-two of their twenty-nine triumphs. In the first three, the results were of little importance, but there is no one who would deny the rôle which the 1916 Democratic triumph in California, Washington, North Dakota, Kansas, and New Mexico played in the outcome of that spectacular election.

The Border section presents a curious picture. Before 1896, the Republicans had won only two out of eighteen close contests, and none of the thirteen between 1880 and 1896. But beginning with the fusionist election, this party outscored the Democrats by taking forty-five of the seventy-seven contests. In 1896 and 1924, the Republicans took all six, and three of the five in 1900.

The South needs little comment. From 1880 to 1916, the Democrats took all sixteen 10 per cent contests. Before 1880, the Republicans had taken ten of thirteen, and since 1920, they have won in six of the nine. No state of the deep South contributed a contest to this category from 1888 to 1924, which reveals something of the consistent Democratic preponderance in those seven states.

Non-Majority Contests

A consideration of those contests in which no party received an absolute majority of the popular votes, and which thereby gave the electoral votes to the plurality winners, is essentially a study of the formal effect of third parties in our national politics. Of the 812 elections, only 112, or 13.8 per cent, have been won by less than a majority. Third parties were no real factor from 1864 to 1876, and during this period there was only one non-majority contest (Indiana in 1876). From 1880 to 1936, there were 111 such contests in the 675 elections (16.4 per cent). And from 1888 to 1924, there were ninety-nine out of 455 contests, or 21.8 per cent. This period includes the three great third-party campaigns—1892, 1912, and 1924. In these three elections alone, sixty-five of the 112 non-majority contests (58.1 per cent) occurred.

But 1916 had eleven, 1888 ten, 1908 eight, and 1884 five such contests.[10]

In 1900 there were no non-majority contests; in 1904, 1920, 1928, and 1936 only one each; in 1932 only two; and in 1896 only three. Thus, before 1924 the Republicans won the not-too-close contests, while the four elections won by the Democrats produced sixty-seven, or 60 per cent, of the 112 non-majority contests. The inevitable conclusion is that during this period the Democrats profited materially from third parties. The third-party election of 1924 was more detrimental to the Democrats than to the Coolidge-led Republicans, and the landslide Democratic victories of 1932 and 1936 were conclusive in themselves and were not the result of third-party campaigns. On the other hand, the tremendous Roosevelt majorities were enhanced by the absence of strong third-party movements.

With these observations, it is well to turn to a consideration of the party distribution of these non-majority tri-

[10] The distribution and winners of non-majority contests were as follows:

Section	1864-76		1880-1892			1896-1916			1920-1936			1864-1936		
	R.	D.	R.	D.	M.	R.	D.	M.	R.	D.	M.	R.	D.	M.
East			2	7		2	8	1	1	2		5	17	1
Border				4		3	7		4	1		7	12	
South														
Mid. West		1	10	4		4	5	2		1	1	14	11	3
West			6	2	1	5	18	1	9			20	20	2
U. S.		1	18	17	1	14	38	4	14	4	1	46	60	6

umphs. Of the 112, the Republicans won forty-six; the Democrats, sixty; and third parties, six. In 1884 the Democrats won four of the five contests, in 1892 eight of the eighteen, in 1912 twenty-six of the thirty-three, and in 1916 four of eleven, but in 1924 they lost every one of the fourteen non-majority contests. Thus, in the four elections in which the Democrats received a majority in the electoral college, they triumphed in forty-two of the sixty-seven plurality contests (62.7 per cent).

None of the twelve southern states has ever cast an electoral vote that did not have a majority of the popular votes behind it. This reveals the fact that strong third-party movements there swallow the trickle of Republican votes at the outset, before they invade the dominant Democratic ranks. Third parties in the South have little effect upon the size of Democratic majorites and no effect upon the certainty of them.

Of the twenty-three non-majority contests in the east, eighteen came in the six campaigns of Democratic national triumph. Of these, the Democrats won fourteen. Of the other five, in years of Republican success, the Democrats won three, two of which were in New Jersey, a consistently Democratic state before 1896. In the Border states, only eight of the nineteen were in years of Democratic national success, but the Democrats won seven of them. Of the other eleven, the Republicans took six, four of which were in 1924. In the Middle West, the Republicans won just half of the twenty-eight non-majority contests, but the Progressives of 1912 and 1924 took three. Of the eleven Democratic triumphs, ten occurred in years of Democratic success, and of these, five occurred in 1912. The other was in 1876 when Indiana voted for Governor Tilden. Fourteen of the twenty Democratic triumphs in the West were in years of national party success, and ten of them were in 1912, when the Republicans carried but one western state. Nine of the Republicans' twenty victories were in 1924, when LaFollette polled his amazing vote in that section.

Sectional Hegemony and the Electoral College

There is, perhaps, nothing more futile than an electoral vote cast for a losing candidate. It is doubly unimportant because the outcome of the national election is known far in advance of the electoral college balloting. At best, it is no more than a belated protest. Though no more than a majority is required in the electoral college, the winning majorities in the nineteen elections have accounted for 72 per cent of the total electoral votes. Through a set of curious circumstances, the Republicans have utilized 85.2 per cent of their total number of electoral votes, while the Democratic efficiency has been but 57.2 per cent. This strange fact results from the almost complete absence of Republican electors in 1912, 1932, and 1936. In those three elections they secured but seventy-five electoral votes. Their only serious loss of electoral votes was in 1916 when they received 254. On the other hand, only since 1872 have the Democrats polled less than one hundred votes. That was in 1928 when the "solid" South was conspicuously gelatinous.

Though the state is the intermediate unit in the electoral college process, the great political movements that elect and defeat candidates for the presidency are surprisingly sectional in scope. The larger clashes in the electoral college are therefore intersectional rather than intrasectional. In the nineteen elections, thirteen Republican and six Democratic victories have been recorded. Yet three sections have cast more than 70 per cent of their electoral votes for winning candidates. And, of these, the Middle West has lost but 14.29 per cent of its total electoral count. In only one election (1916) has that section, since 1884, failed to cast a majority of its electoral vote for the winning candidate. And 1884 was the only other election in which that politically astute section failed to support the winner.

Thus, while the Middle West has won seventeen of the nineteen elections, the South, on the other extreme, has lost in nine of eighteen.[11] Two of these nine southern victories were in 1868 and 1872, when under the leadership of carpet baggers the section supported General U. S. Grant. Another of these triumphs was that of 1928, when six southern states bolted Governor Smith and thereby gave the Republican candidates a slight majority in the section's electoral count—72 to 64 votes.[12] Being consistently Republican, the East enjoyed fairly regular success, though it lost in 1884, 1892, and 1916. This section did not have the Middle West's propensity for changing political preference. The West's record is spotted, and, before 1920, the section had less unanimity of opinion than the other four regions. The Border has a curious record. Before 1896, it was dissentient; afterwards it climbed on the bandwagon.

The World War represents a period in which the American people did things on a grand scale, and in which they visual-

---

[11] The South did not participate in 1864, and only eight southern states took part in the 1868 contest.

[12] Virginia, North Carolina, Tennessee, Florida, Texas, and Oklahoma cast Republican electoral votes. For Texas, this was her "first offense," but all others had, in one or two elections, voted Republican.

THE ELECTORAL COLLEGE

ized an extension of that grandiosity. In the five post-war elections, 83.8 per cent of the total electoral vote was cast for successful candidates. From 1864 to 1916, only 65.27 per cent went to victors. In other words, the ratio of dissent in the electoral college before the World War was more than twice that of the post-war period.

This latter period marks a new development in national politics. During it, both parties have been fairly evenly balanced and each badly routed in individual elections. In it, there has occurred one of the country's most spectacular third-party campaigns and an election in which the third-party vote was indeed negligible. Whole sections have shifted with the political winds. For instance, the West, though casting 427 electoral votes in the five elections, wasted not a single vote—a "grand slam" in political clairvoyance! And the Middle West had a record almost as impressive. Of 607 electoral votes, 594 went to winners. Only Wisconsin missed and in only one election (1924), when she showed her appreciation for the long political leadership of her senior senator. Records of the five sections are shown in TABLE 17.

An examination of the complete record of the five sections proves interesting. The efficacy of the Middle West is amazing. The loss of only 14.29 per cent of its 2,060 electors constitutes a remarkable record, especially since it participated fully in that period of bitter partisan struggle from the Civil War to Populist-Democratic fusion. During this era, the Middle West lost but 20.7 per cent while the mark for the entire United States was 35.7 per cent. Thus it exceeded the entire country by 23.3 per cent in efficiency of selecting the winner. And if its votes be considered apart, it exceeded the other four section's mark by 34.9 per cent.

In the first four elections (1864-1876), the fifteen votes of Indiana in 1876 were the only losing ones. All voted for Garfield and Harrison (1888), but Indiana supported Cleveland in 1884. However, in Cleveland's third presidential

TABLE 17.—SECTIONAL EFFECTIVENESS IN THE ELECTORAL COLLEGE BY PERIODS

Section	1864-1876		1880-1892		1896-1916	
	Used	Wasted	Used	Wasted	Used	Wasted
East	338	97	305	151	589	179
Border	47	113	93	89	195	97
South	107	123	219	202	272	471
Middle West	331	15	271	142	570	124
West	70	3	55	87	306	112
United States	893	351	943	671	1932	975

Section	1920-1936		1864-1936			
			Number		Percentage	
	Used	Wasted	Used	Wasted	Used	Wasted
East	578	87	1848	514	78.24	21.76
Border	224	16	559	315	63.96	36.04
South	364	314	962	1110	46.43	53.57
Middle West	594	13	1766	294	85.71	14.29
West	427		858	202	80.94	19.06
United States	2187	430	5993	2435	70.94	29.06

campaign, Indiana was joined by Illinois and Wisconsin and by six scattering electors from Ohio and Michigan. The next four elections found every middle western electoral vote cast for the winning Republican nominees, but in 1912 Michigan and Minnesota supported the Bull Moose insurgency; and in

THE ELECTORAL COLLEGE

1916, only Ohio saved her vote in Wilson's re-election. Next to that of 1884, this was the worst defeat of the Middle West during the long period. If these two elections are excluded, the section's mark of efficiency for the other seventeen contests is 93.5 per cent.

Ohio, the most effective state of the section, has not backed a loser since 1896, and in that year she gave only one vote to Bryan. Excluding 1916, Iowa has not failed since 1892, Illinois since 1884, and Indiana since 1876. Wisconsin's misses were in 1884, 1916, and 1924; Minnesota and Michigan lost in 1884, 1892, 1912, and 1916, though the latter gave five of her fourteen votes to Cleveland in 1892.

With 23 per cent of the national electoral votes, the seven states of the Middle West represent the most vital force in the election of presidents, because the section has voted as a unit in thirteen of the nineteen elections, and in three of those six split contests, only one state was in disagreement.[13] Thus, in 84.2 per cent of the elections, the section was in substantial agreement, and in 68.4 per cent in unanimous decision.[14] The political superiority of the Middle West is shown in *Figure 7*. Naturally, the section's percentage of efficiency has been well above that of the entire country. Though highest in but one period (1896-1916), it has never been lower than second place in the efficiency standings.

The West is the second most prescient section, though most of its votes were cast in the last half of the period under consideration. Here there occurs the stunning phenomenon of states which have never lost an electoral vote. Both New

[13] Indiana in 1876 and 1884, and Wisconsin in 1924.
[14] In 1892, the count was 57 to 53 with Cleveland leading; in 1912, it was 94 to 27 with Wilson ahead; but in 1916 it was 97 for Hughes against Ohio's 24 votes for Wilson.

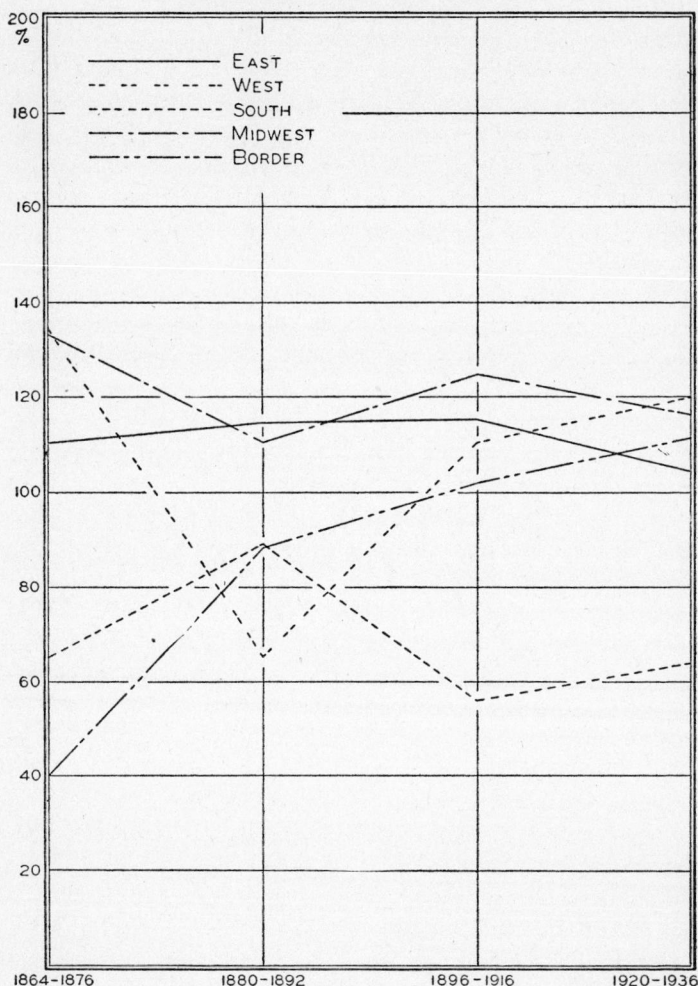

Figure 7.—*Sectional Percentages of National Vote Effectiveness*

THE ELECTORAL COLLEGE

Mexico and Arizona have been with the majority in the last seven elections—four Democratic and three Republican. And North Dakota has lost but two of her fifty votes, both of which came in her initial election (1892) and before she was fully oriented into the ways of picking a successful ticket. At least she achieved 100 per cent efficiency from 1896 to 1936. Only Ohio has a longer period of consecutive political successes.

The second period was the poorest for the West. Her record of efficiency was seriously reduced by the failure to cast a single electoral vote for Cleveland in 1884 and by giving him only nine of fifty-seven in 1892. Nevada lost 75 per cent of her votes in these four elections, Nebraska 62 per cent, Kansas 58 per cent, Colorado 54 per cent, Oregon 50 per cent, and California 45 per cent. Of the twenty votes polled by the five states, which in 1892 participated for the first time in national elections, fifteen were given to the losing Harrison.

After 1896, the West jumped back above the national efficiency average, though her faith in Bryan was enough to give him seventy-five losing votes in his three races. Colorado and Nevada supported him in all three races, Nebraska and Montana in two, and South Dakota, Kansas, Wyoming, Utah, and Washington in one each. The record of South Dakota is interesting. In three of the six elections, she lost her electoral vote, one of which was given to the Democrats, one to the Republicans, and one to the Bull Moose faction. Washington also supported all three of these parties during the period, but she lost only twice. As before stated, since 1920, the section has not lost an electoral vote, which sets a new all-time record for sectional political prescience.

As the most consistent, though only third in effectiveness, the East has been too strongly Republican to follow when the remainder of the country has gone Democratic. However, in none of the four periods has the section been below the national mark for effectiveness. Even in 1884 and 1892 enough states broke to the Cleveland standard to retain the above-average percentage of effectiveness. New York, New Jersey, and Connecticut were Democratic in both these elections. The other six states were rock-ribbed Republican baronies from which not a Democratic elector was selected from 1864 until 1912. Thus, these five New England states and Pennsylvania polled 762 Republican electoral votes before they "disgraced" themselves and their section by contributing thirty-three votes to Wilson's 1912 total. But in 1916, the entire section, except for New Hampshire's four lonely electors, was again in the Republican column. After the World War the monotony of Republican success was broken only by the action of Massachusetts and Rhode Island in voting for Smith in 1928. And four years later, New York and New Jersey joined them in the revolt against Mr. Hoover, but the five others stayed firm, giving the President his electoral total except for three stray electors from Delaware. In 1936, the Republicans carried only Vermont and Maine.

Of the nine states, New Hampshire and New York have been most efficient in escaping loss of electoral votes. The former has failed three times—1884, 1892, and 1932. New York missed in 1868, 1876, and 1916. The least effective were the most thoroughly Republican—Vermont and Pennsylvania. Thus, while Connecticut and New Jersey lost in the Reconstruction period by going Democratic, they have pulled up their average since 1896 by breaking from the Republicans in the years of Democratic success. Both Massachusetts and Rhode Island are states that have since 1920 moved across the line from a safe Republican to a plurality Democratic position.

The Border presents a curious record. For the first two periods it was below the national average; for the last two it was above. The strong Democratic tradition there brought loss of electoral votes in the early period, but the official infusion of radicalism into the Democratic party in 1896 was reflected by Republican victories in the section. In the second period the section won four more votes than it lost (93 to 89) to contrast with the forty-seven winning Republican and the 113 losing Democratic electors of the first four elections. In the third period, the Border lost only ninety-seven of 292 votes. Kentucky was the only state with fewer effective than wasted electoral votes during this period. Since 1920, reflecting the general political attitude of the country, the Border has lost but sixteen of 240 votes. West Virginia has been the most effective state, missing only in 1876, 1880, 1888, and 1916. She voted Republican in eleven elections, and Democratic in eight. Kentucky has been too Democratic to be effective and she lost 124 electors to the 112 which she cast for winners. She voted Republican in 1896, 1924, and 1928. The percentages of the other three states were, in the sixties, close to the Border and the national averages.

The South has been the stepchild in national politics since the Civil War. It has been forced to rationalize being right rather than successful. Wasting 53.5 per cent of its total electoral vote, it has had only one period (1920-1936) in which it has cast more winners than losers (365 to 314), and this was made possible only by the revolt against Smith in 1928. From 1880 to 1916, the section cast not a single Republican electoral vote. The youngest state of the South, Oklahoma, leads the other eleven in effectiveness, winning six of her eight elections, losing only in 1908 and 1924. On the other extreme is Georgia, which has never cast a Republican electoral vote, and has, therefore, six winning and twelve losing elections. She matches Vermont, which was exclusively Republican. These are the only states of the forty-eight with records of absolute party consistency. Of the other ten states, only North Carolina and Florida have contributed more winning than losing votes, and they are barely on the majority side. The percentages of the other eight are in the forties.

Individual States and Effectiveness in the Electoral College

So much has already been said of the state records that little further discussion is necessary. Yet states do not always follow their sections and for that reason they should be considered as the political entities which they are. For purposes of brevity, the states and their percentage of effectiveness are listed in order in TABLE 18. A careful examination of the table reveals clearly the part which sections play in the clash of major parties. In the upper quartile, comprising the states that shift from one party to another, lie the twelve states that select presidents. In 1936, these twelve polled 178 electoral votes, or more than one-third of the total electoral vote.

The upper-quartile states have been essentially Republican

in politics, but the minority party has been sufficiently strong to come to power with the assistance of independent voters. In the nineteen elections, 70.23 per cent of their electors have been Republican. This is only slightly above the percentage of Republican success in the seventy-two years. Of their Republican electoral votes, 87.55 per cent have been cast for

TABLE 18.—EFFECTIVENESS OF INDIVIDUAL STATES IN THE ELECTORAL COLLEGE

Rank State	Elections	Electoral Votes Eff.	Electoral Votes Wasted	% Eff.	Rank State	Elections	Electoral Votes Eff.	Electoral Votes Wasted	% Eff.
1. N. M.	7	21	0	100.	25. Minn.	19	128	40	76.2
2. Ariz.	7	21	0	100.	26. Me.	19	89	28	76.1
3. N. D.	12	48	2	96.	27. Neb.	18	87	29	75.
4. Ohio	19	396	45	89.8	28. N. J.	19	160	55	74.4
5. Ind.	19	249	30	89.7	29. Colo.	16	56	20	73.7
6. Ill.	19	417	51	89.1	30. Vt.	19	57	22	72.2
7. Cal.	19	174	26	87.	31. Pa.	19	451	174	72.2
8. N. H.	19	79	12	85.2	32. Mo.	19	211	95	68.9
9. N. Y.	19	635	113	84.9	33. Nev.	19	38	18	67.1
10. Wyo.	12	30	6	83.3	34. S. D.	12	35	18	66.
11. Wis.	19	182	37	83.1	35. Md.	19	98	52	65.3
12. Ia.	19	188	39	82.8	36. Del.	19	36	21	63.2
13. Utah	11	33	7	82.5	37. Fla.	17	48	38	55.8
14. W. Va.	19	102	23	81.6	38. N. C.	18	103	101	50.5
15. Kan.	19	128	29	81.5	39. Tenn.	18	104	108	49.1
16. Ore.	19	61	14	81.3	40. Texas	17	134	143	48.4
17. Mich.	19	206	52	79.8	41. S. C.	18	72	79	47.7
18. Wash.	12	58	15	79.4	42. Ken.	19	112	124	47.5
19. Mont.	12	34	9	79.1	43. Va.	17	93	106	46.7
20. Idaho	12	34	9	79.1	44. Ala.	18	85	110	43.6
21. Okla.	8	62	17	78.5	45. La.	17	64	87	42.4
22. Conn.	19	97	27	78.2	46. Ark.	17	56	80	41.2
23. Mass.	19	227	65	77.7	47. Miss.	17	64	93	40.8
24. R. I.	19	63	18	77.7	48. Ga.	18	77	148	34.2

winning candidates. But there is another point that is important. Though each of the twelve states has, from three to seven times, gone Democratic, as a unit they have lost but 11.42 per cent of their total Democratic poll. Eight of the twelve states have never lost a Democratic electoral vote.[15] Of the other four, New York has lost 24.37 per cent of her Democratic electors,[16] Wyoming 20 per cent, Indiana 17.05 per cent,[17] and California 8.22 per cent. From 1880 to 1936 these twelve states lost only nine of 723 Democratic electors, for an efficiency mark of 98.77 per cent.[18] This proves the essential Republican convictions of these twelve states. As a group, the members of this quartile are moderate third-party states, though not leaders in that respect. The leading Populist states are in the lower quartiles. Only California gave electors to Theodore Roosevelt in 1912, and she split the delegation between him and Wilson. To summarize, the obvious truth may be pointed out, that these are the plastic states, the close political states, where the Democrats have had a good chance of winning whenever the Republican house was not in the best of order.

The second quartile comprises a veritable hodgepodge. All sections are represented, though the West claims six of the places. These western states were Populist strongholds that were favorable to fusion.[19] But there are consistent Republican states here—Michigan, Massachusetts, and Rhode

[15] New Mexico, Arizona, North Dakota, Ohio, Illinois, New Hampshire, Wisconsin, and Iowa.

[16] All of New York's Democratic electoral loss came before 1880. Her support of two of her former governors (1868 and 1876) cost her sixty-eight electoral votes.

[17] Indiana's only losing Democratic vote was in 1876.

[18] California lost five Democratic electors in 1880 and one in 1896, and Wyoming lost three in 1896.

[19] Oregon is an exception.

Island, along with Oregon, which voted for that party in years of Democratic national success.[20] Here also is the late comer, Oklahoma, the prescient Border demesne of West Virginia, and the changeable Connecticut, which lost with the Democrats too often before 1896 to win a high efficiency rating.

The third quartile comprises states of three categories. First, there are the Republican bailiwicks—Vermont, Pennsylvania, Maine, Minnesota, and Nebraska. Second, there are the great Populist strongholds—Colorado, Missouri, South Dakota, and Nevada.[21] Third, there march here the states which have definitely shifted their allegiance from one party to the other—New Jersey, Maryland, and Delaware.[22] Here exists indisputable refutation of the long heralded Republican slogan—"As Maine goes, so goes the nation!" From the point of political effectiveness, Maine ranks twenty-sixth of the forty-eight states. Ohio, Indiana, or Illinois would have been far more efficient presagers, but not so effective for Republican educational purposes, as the early elections in Maine and her persistent Republican decisions were good material for Republican propaganda.

The fourth quartile needs no comment. Every state is Democratic and has quite consistently followed that party, for better or for worse, since the passing of the carpet baggers. Kentucky is the only non-southern state in the group, but

[20] All went Republican in 1884, 1892, and 1916, though Michigan split in 1892.

[21] Populism was also strong in Nebraska and of some importance in Minnesota, though both of these states were consistently Republican.

[22] The placing of three Border states (Maryland, Delaware, and Missouri) in this quartile is not mere accident. From their earlier Democratic leanings, they crossed to the Republicans after 1892. New Jersey and Connecticut followed much the same route; they might well be classed as Border states but for geographic factors.

her geographic proximity to that section and her Democratic propensities kept her on the losing side in the long stretches of Republican rule. Her only Republican aberrations were those of 1896, 1924, and 1928.

Wasted Popular Votes

In the pages immediately preceding, the effectiveness of states in picking winners in the electoral college has been under consideration. There is no intention of preaching a doctrine of "nothing succeeds like success." It is the stu-

TABLE 19.—WASTED POPULAR VOTES: BY PERIODS, SECTIONS, AND PARTIES

Section	1864-1876					
	Republican	%	Democratic	%	Others	%
East	1,212,495	25.1	3,198,385	78.5	17,226	100.
Border	754,516	71.8	200,530	15.3	14,701	100.
South	834,236	43.8	761,114	34.9	7,021	100.
M. W.	208,011	4.5	3,468,254	94.2	70,276	100.
West	10,961	2.1	363,994	97.9	14,024	100.
U. S.	2,020,219	15.8	7,992,277	68.8	123,248	100.

Section	1880-1892					
	Republican	%	Democratic	%	Others	%
East	1,933,484	29.3	4,033,378	68.2	388,676	100.
Border	1,958,469	97.2	67,152	2.8	187,518	100.
South	2,767,771	100.			390,836	100.
M. W.	1,064,541	15.7	4,429,175	72.1	626,758	100.
West	215,249	12.0	891,165	79.8	341,869	57.7
U. S.	7,939,514	39.8	9,420,870	46.6	1,935,656	88.6

THE ELECTORAL COLLEGE

Section	1896-1916					
	Republican	%	Democratic	%	Others	%
East	1,192,816	9.0	8,506,683	86.3	1,673,481	76.1
Border	2,400,627	52.8	1,709,191	36.7	598,037	100.
South	3,322,545	100.0			479,526	100.
M. W.	1,664,839	11.4	9,760,942	82.5	2,250,732	85.2
West	2,214,209	37.6	1,966,942	32.9	1,109,882	65.7
U. S.	10,795,036	25.9	21,943,758	55.2	6,111,658	79.3

Section	1920-1936						1864-1936		
	Republican	%	Democratic	%	Others	%	R. %	D. %	Oth %
East	10,218,069	35.4	10,386,129	43.0	2,595,585	100.	27.4	58.4	89.5
Border	3,608,470	41.7	4,024,450	42.7	365,665	100.	53.6	33.2	100.0
South	3,875,465	70.1	1,678,903	12.8	370,862	100.0	79.3	8.8	100.0
M. W.	11,508,226	39.2	8,892,683	38.4	3,342,981	95.6	26.1	59.8	87.6
West	5,107,089	37.4	3,921,974	31.7	2,086,306	100.0	34.6	36.0	81.1
United States	34,317,319	39.5	28,904,139	34.9	8,761,399	98.5	35.0	44.2	88.3

dent's task to discover "who governs America." Another phase of the problem is the popular-vote wastage in the choice of electors. A wasted popular vote is one that did not directly aid in the selection of an elector. Thus those popular votes which lay behind electors who were in the minority in the electoral college are not, by this definition, wasted votes, for they assisted directly in the choice of electors. To achieve brevity, this important phenomenon of the American political system will be considered only from the point of view of the entire period. The figures are shown in TABLE 19.

The East has been consistently harsh to the Democrats.

PRESIDENTIAL ELECTIONS

In no period have the wasted votes of the Republicans equaled those of the Democrats. In the first period, the Democratic percentage of wastage was three times that of their successful rivals; in the second it was two and one-half times greater; in the third it was more than nine times greater; and in the last, even with two unprecedented Democratic landslides, it was more than one-fourth higher. The lowest of all percentages of Democratic wastage was in New Jersey,[23] while every Democratic vote in Vermont was futile. From 1864 to 1884, six of the nine states destroyed the efficacy of every Democratic popular vote. This accounts for the high mortality rate for that party during the first two periods—78.5 per cent and 68.2 per cent. And the third period followed with an even higher amount of wastage with 86.3 per cent. The tremendous shift of eastern votes from the Republicans to the Democrats in the last two elections of the contemporary period reduced the losses of the Democrats and boosted those of the Republicans, as the large Progressive vote did in 1912. The Republican schism of the latter campaign nullified all

[23] The wastage figures for the nine eastern states were:

State	Republican	Democrat	Others	Total
Maine	1.5	95.2	100.0	39.9
New Hampshire	15.8	79.2	100.0	45.5
Vermont	0.0	100.0	100.0	31.8
Massachusetts	38.1	45.3	100.0	44.4
Rhode Island	40.1	43.3	100.0	43.9
Connecticut	25.5	53.5	100.0	40.4
New York	35.4	51.7	100.0	46.1
New Jersey	40.2	42.1	100.0	43.5
Pennsylvania	12.3	78.7	63.8	42.2
Total East	27.4	58.4	89.5	43.9

THE ELECTORAL COLLEGE

Taft votes except the few in Vermont. For the nineteen elections, the Democrats lost over twenty-five million of their almost forty-four million total votes, or 58.4 per cent. On the other hand, the Republicans lost only 27.4 per cent of their 53,464,623 votes. The minor party loss was 89.5 per cent. This reveals the great diasdvantage under which the Democrats have operated in the East. They have lost 25,705,575 votes to only 14,641,486 Republican ones. Third parties have secured only thirty-eight electoral votes with their 5,227,751 total votes, for a loss or over four and one-half million. Third parties saved only the vote in Pennsylvania in 1912. They lost those of the other 170 contests.

The Border treated the Republicans uncharitably before 1896, wasting 88.5 per cent of their more than three million votes. After 1896, their loss was but 45.6 per cent as compared with the corresponding Democratic loss of 40 per cent. This proves the fundamental reorientation of political allegiance in this fingerling section. However, as a whole, the Democratic loss of 33.2 per cent is appreciably smaller than the 53.6 per cent of the Republicans for the period. Delaware has been most favorable to the Republicans and Kentucky to the Democrats.[24]

[24] The percentages of waste in the Border were:

State	Republican	Democrat	Others	Total
Delaware	19.4	73.0	100.0	46.2
Maryland	47.4	35.1	100.0	43.1
West Virginia	38.0	49.7	100.0	44.1
Kentucky	71.9	15.6	100.0	43.3
Missouri	53.4	35.6	100.0	45.8
Total Border	53.6	33.2	100.0	44.8

PRESIDENTIAL ELECTIONS

If the electoral college has militated against the Democrats in the East, it has been equally unfair to the Republicans in the South. Of the 14,629,968 wasted southern votes, 74.5 per cent have been Republican and only 16.3 per cent Democratic, as contrasted to the East's record of 32.5 per cent Republican, and 57.1 per cent Democratic wasted votes. Democratic apologists have little to deprecate except the limited population and geographic extent of the South. By nullifying every Republican vote, Georgia led the section, but Arkansas had a mark of 92.1 per cent, Tennessee 91.2 per cent, Alabama 85.4 per cent, and Virginia 84 per cent. On the contrary, Georgia saved every Democrat vote, while Arkansas wasted but 1.4 per cent of her total, Mississippi 3.4 per cent, and Louisiana 4 per cent.[25] Though these figures are unnecessary to prove the historical accuracy of the "Solid South" label, they are nevertheless essential to the understanding of the operation of the electoral-college system. For

[25] The percentage losses of the twelve southern states were as follows:

State	Republican	Democrat	Others	Total
Virginia	84.0	9.8	100.0	41.1
North Carolina	79.3	11.8	100.0	39.4
Tennessee	91.2	14.3	100.0	46.6
South Carolina	37.8	13.4	100.0	19.7
Georgia	100.0	0.0	100.0	29.5
Florida	65.7	6.5	100.0	33.4
Alabama	85.4	7.2	100.0	34.2
Mississippi	73.2	3.4	100.0	20.1
Louisiana	73.5	4.0	100.0	21.5
Arkansas	92.1	1.4	100.0	34.5
Texas	77.3	6.7	100.0	28.2
Oklahoma	60.0	20.7	100.0	40.4
Total South	79.3	8.8	100.0	34.6

THE ELECTORAL COLLEGE

if the South were to demand a proportional formula for the distribution of electoral votes, the other sections would have an indisputable moral right to demand the reform of the election laws and the discriminatory practices of the South.

Next to the Border, the Middle West had the highest rate of wastage, which means that the elections were won by smaller margins than in the South, East, or West. For the period, 44.1 per cent of the total vote was wasted; of this wastage 56.7 per cent was Democratic, 30.6 per cent Republican, and 12.6 per cent of minor parties. In the contemporary period the Democratic loss decreased precipitously from the highs of the first three, and that of the Republicans consequently increased. In the last two elections, the Republicans lost almost eleven million votes in the section. Of the seven middle western states, Iowa treated the Republicans most, and the Democrats least, favorably. Wisconsin was better to the Democrats and Indiana harshest to the Republicans.[26] The section had the lowest Republican wastage percentage of any of the other four and at the same time contributed the highest mark against the Democrats.

[26] The percentages of waste in the Middle West were:

State	Republican	Democrat	Others	Total
Ohio	26.0	57.4	100.0	43.6
Indiana	30.9	59.3	100.0	46.9
Michigan	22.1	57.8	70.7	38.8
Illinois	28.6	62.3	100.0	47.0
Wisconsin	29.5	54.5	51.1	42.2
Minnesota	24.4	62.2	82.3	44.3
Iowa	18.2	66.1	100.0	42.8
Total Middle West	26.1	59.8	87.6	44.1

Illinois negatived more than seven million Democratic votes, Ohio more than six million, and Indiana more than four million. In fact, the total Democratic wastage in these three states exceeded that of the Republicans in the twelve southern states—another evidence of the key political position held by the Middle West.

As shown before, the West is a mercurial section. It shifts its allegiance from one to another of the great parties, and on occasions spends considerable time in the half-way station of third parties. On account of this promiscuity in party allegiance, it is the only section that wasted less than 50 per cent of the votes of both major parties. The marks of 34.6 per cent for the Republicans and 36 per cent for the Democrats emphasize its propensity for practical politics. Since it is the newest section, only six of the fifteen states passed through the post-Civil-War period of close and persistent party allegiance. As shown by the states of the other sections, these stubborn allegiances that persisted until 1896 resulted in the wholesale wastage of Republican votes in the Border and South and of the Democratic votes in the East and Middle West. The latter sections were more populous and therefore retained fairly regular possession of the presidency.

After 1896, those loyalties faded before the rising problems of the ripening industrialism. Economic security of the individual became of more importance than the retention of the heroism of Manassas Junction or Antietam. The epic was replaced by the realistic. Administrations that came to power with the mandates of tremendous majorities were unceremoniously defeated by equally tremendous majorities. The new West was born in the early part of this innovative era, and it reflected that uncertainty in its political affiliations. An unpopular candidate could reduce a party poll in the section by 25 per cent, as Judge Parker did in 1904 and as John W. Davis did in 1924. President Hoover's 1932 poll was almost one-third under that of 1928. Therefore, the record of the West must be interpreted in the light of this recent trend in American politics, a trend that promises to make parties more amenable to the immediately vital problems of social maladjustments.

The West has come to epitomize the new realism in American politics. An election is not a party battle—it is a crusade. The whole section—as a unit—moves with decision. Politics is a serious business. It is no mere preliminary to a public triumph, when the winners may march to receive the plaudits of citizens. The West is an amateur in politics. It has no interest in keeping opponents in the game merely to perpetuate the sport. Thus, a party's fortunes may rise very high, only to fall to the lowest depths in the next election. The nine newer western states, those which were not participants before 1892, show this recent trend. They have negatived 12 per cent more Republican votes per thousand, almost 2 per cent less Democratic ballots, and 8 per cent more of total votes than the six older states of the section. This means that third parties have been of more importance, and that the Democrats have been stronger since 1892 than during the seven elections preceding that year.

Of the fifteen states, Oregon has been most favorable to the Republicans and harshest to the Democrats. On the other hand, Colorado has wasted 48.3 per cent of her total Republican vote, while Washington has negatived but 28.2 per cent of her Democratic vote. Colorado politics for twenty years reflected the influence of Populism. On the whole, the wastage records of the fifteen states follow a very general pattern.[27] There is less disparity between the two parties, for this section epitomizes fairly accurately the clash between the other four sections. It stands less firmly behind a party than the other sections do, though the majority which a party receives in the West in a particular election may be as large as that of any other section. For instance, Hoover's western percentage in 1928 was over three percentage points above that of any other section and yet, in 1932, only the South exceeded the West in support of Franklin D. Roosevelt.

A summary of the foregoing discussion on wastage of party votes in the various sections can best be presented in tabular form.

The largest Republican wastages have occurred in the

[27] The wastage figures for the fifteen western states were:

State	Republican	Democrat	Others	Total
North Dakota	36.2	42.2	99.5	45.4
South Dakota	28.6	43.6	73.5	40.1
Nebraska	37.3	40.4	100.0	43.8
Kansas	36.3	45.5	73.4	43.0
Montana	40.5	32.6	100.0	42.7
Idaho	42.8	31.3	92.4	43.1
Wyoming	39.1	35.4	100.0	43.1
Colorado	48.3	28.7	81.5	41.7
Utah	31.8	45.2	100.0	42.8
New Mexico	44.4	35.8	100.0	43.3
Arizona	40.9	31.0	100.0	39.2
Nevada	40.0	37.5	78.6	42.1
California	27.8	29.0	70.4	32.3
Oregon	23.6	54.1	100.0	43.9
Washington	39.0	28.2	73.4	39.7
Total West	34.6	36.0	81.1	39.6

Border, South, and West, with the least in the Middle West, and with the East in the middle ground. The Democrats fared poorly in the Middle West and East, well in the South and West, with the Border section between the extremes. The Border and South have shown no favor at all to third parties and the East very little, while the Middle West and West have been their only fairly successful areas. Interestingly enough,

TABLE 20.—SECTIONAL WASTAGE RECORDS IN RELATION TO NATIONAL AVERAGES

Section	National Rep. Average		National Dem. Aver.		National 3rd party Average		National Total party's Aver.	
	States below	States above	States below	States above	States below	States above	States below	States above
East	5	4	2	7	1	8	4	5
Border	1	4	3	2	0	5	0	5
South	0	12	12	0	0	12	11	1
Middle West	7	0	0	7	3	4	2	5
West	4	11	12	3	6	9	7	8
United States	17	31	29	19	10	38	24	24

in total wastage, there were twenty-four states on each side of the national average, but only the South had a majority of states below that average. This results from the one-party system that operates in that section. Where strong rivalry exists between the two major parties, the popular vote wastage inevitably increases. Thus, each of the other four sections had a majority of states above the national average, though the collective mark of the West was below. Of the fifteen western states, twelve were within a 10 per cent variation from the national average. The other three were below it, which reduced the section's average below the national one, even though there were eight states above and only seven states below.

★ ★ ★ ★ ★

CHAPTER FIVE

Geography of Decision

★ ★ ★ ★ ★ ★ ★ ★

IN the preceding discussion, attention has been focused upon the choice of electors as an end in itself. The selection of a Democratic elector was a victory for that party, even though he was united with but twenty others of his kind, as in 1864, and opposed in the electoral college by an overwhelming majority of Republican electors. In the immediately succeeding pages, the point of discussion shifts to the consideration of the effectiveness of popular votes, to the real decision-making element in the election, to those popular votes which lie behind the winning electoral-college majority.

By this definition of effectiveness, all wasted votes (votes cast for a losing candidate for the electoral college) are joined to those votes cast for winning electors of a losing party. Thus, in 1916, only 43,781 Democratic votes of the 4,437,928 total votes of the East, would be accredited as effective votes, for New Hampshire was the only eastern state that cast its electoral vote for the re-election of Woodrow Wilson. Thus, all Republican votes were ineffective, and all Democratic votes, with this single exception, and all third-party votes were wasted. For this election, then, the East's percentage of effectiveness was just under one per cent.

The percentage of effectiveness is suprisingly low until after 1920, the period of landslide majorities. The effective portion of the almost one hundred and fifty-six million total votes from 1864 to 1916 was only 37.41 per cent, as against 46.76 per cent for the period between 1920 and 1936. This last mercurial period represents an increase of 25 per cent in the ratio of effectiveness. And still there are those who will not admit that the party system has recently passed, and is now passing, through one of the most fundamental revolutions of its entire history. Moreover, it is not so much the party system itself that is being affected. Rather it is the spirit that lies beneath it, which motivates it, and gives it being. Party labels may change, party programs may be put forth with all the ponderous ostentation of the past, but the crispness with which electorate swings in preponderant majorities is a phenomenon new in American politics. From the very start of an official campaign, there has generally been no doubt of the November winner in any presidential race since 1916.

Are the American people finally achieving a national unity, a common way of life, an organic national ego? One may hear many savants explain this phenomenon in such meaningless phrases as "national mind" or "American public mind." These are mere subjective abstractions. If this "mind" is the result of an election campaign, it is understandable; if it is a monistic, mechanical gadget that moves the people from one problem to another, the concept is inane. The only unity that one perceives is that which derives from the mutuality of problems and the human disposition to react to those problems, in whatever section they may arise, in a manner conducive to individual and social welfare. To a greater

GEOGRAPHY OF DECISION

extent than formerly, American economy is becoming national in scope. Capitalism discovers similar support and opposition in every section, even though the social groups of all sections are not in common political phalanxes. There lies the chief defect to the general observation that the party system is becoming a mere reflection of the development of class consciousness in America.

The tenant farmers of one section may be united with landholders of another, both of whom may be fighting alongside shopkeepers of a third. The great industrialists may be political brothers to those who have lost in the race for worldly goods under the capitalist order. The lines, therefore, are not clearly drawn, even though the voters' decisions may result largely from reaction to economic problems. This seems logically to refute the arguments of economic determinists who ascribe to Marxian dialectics the existing political mores. The American economic order is in the refining process, they remark, and henceforth the people may expect the bitter conflict of economic classes! But modern campaigns are scarcely bitter; rather, they represent great popularity contests, with especial emphasis upon personableness, urbanity, and dramatic appeal. Who was the "forgotten man" of 1932? He could have been anyone in any of the economic groups. He merely epitomized, in dramatic form, anyone who had not received for his talents all that he might have received. And when the New Deal administration implemented its search for the "forgotten man," it found him in every walk of life. It even discriminated, legally, against the forgotten men of different economic levels—a white-collar worker on relief was given a higher wage than the forgotten man from the ranks of unskilled labor!

This phenomenon of overwhelming popular majorities has been noticeable in the five elections since the World War. In thirty-five of the states, a majority of the total popular votes was cast for winning electors.[1] This contrasts strikingly with the six states that exhibited such effective majorities for the period from 1896 to 1916. Almost six times that number of states climbed into the category of plastic politics, in which majorities went to the Republicans in the first three elections and to the Democrats in the last two. In the bitter period from 1880 to 1892, no state had an effective majority for the four elections. The contemporary period is undoubtedly one of loose political allegiance and one in which the citizenry moves in large groups from one party to another.

In the state percentages, Connecticut, twenty-sixth from the top in effectiveness of popular vote, was the first state

[1] The percentages of effective popular votes, (1920-1936), and the ranking of states, are as follows:

First Quartile		Second Quartile		Third Quartile		Fourth Quartile	
1. Mich.	63.8	13. Neb.	59.1	25. Minn.	55.1	37. Del.	45.8
2. Cal.	63.1	14. N. J.	58.7	26. Conn.	54.1	38. R. I.	45.7
3. Ariz.	62.1	15. N. M.	58.4	27. Fla.	53.9	39. N. C.	45.6
4. Nevada	61.6	16. S. D.	57.9	28. Okla.	53.6	40. Ky.	45.5
5. Wash.	60.6	17. Ohio	57.8	29. S. C.	53.3	41. Ga.	44.7
6. Kan.	60.5	18. Mo.	57.4	30. Texas	53.1	42. N. H.	44.2
7. Ore.	60.0	19. Ind.	56.5	31. Miss.	53.1	43. Mass.	44.1
8. Idaho	59.9	20. Md.	56.5	32. N. D.	52.9	44. Va.	43.3
9. Ia.	59.7	21. N. Y.	56.3	33. Wis.	52.5	45. Vt.	39.8
10. Colo.	59.6	22. W. Va.	56.0	34. Tenn.	51.2	46. Ala.	37.9
11. Mont.	59.4	23. Ill.	55.7	35. La.	51.1	47. Ark.	36.6
12. Wyo.	59.1	24. Utah	55.5	36. Penn.	49.7	48. Me.	36.5

GEOGRAPHY OF DECISION

that lost its electoral vote in any one of the five latest elections. Comprising the twenty-five unanimously successful states were fourteen from the West, six from the Middle West, three from the Border, and two from the East. Those twenty-five states cast 289 electoral votes in 1936, which means that their political elasticity is sufficient to win any election wherein they unite. For the five elections they have been unanimous in their ballot decisions!

When vote effectiveness is figured over the entire period from the Civil War, the percentages fall precipitously. Only fourteen states show a complete majority.[2] Of those, nine are western states, only two of which participated in all nineteen elections. The high ratios of effectiveness for the other seven were manifestly boosted by their exceedingly high marks of the contemporary period. Five of the seven held their first presidential elections in 1892, while Arizona and New Mexico were delayed until 1912. Of the thirty-

---

[2] The percentages of effectiveness, and their rankings, are as follows for the period from 1864 to 1936:

First Quartile		Second Quartile		Third Quartile		Fourth Quartile	
1. Ariz.	60.8	13. W. Va.	50.7	25. Ill.	47.9	37. S. C.	43.5
2. Cal.	57.3	14. Ia.	50.5	26. Neb.	47.6	38. Maine	42.1
3. N. M.	56.7	15. Okla.	49.8	27. Vt.	47.5	39. Del.	39.1
4. Wash.	54.1	16. N. J.	49.3	28. Fla.	46.7	40. Miss.	38.9
5. Wyo.	54.0	17. Ind.	49.2	29. Nevada	45.6	41. Texas	38.3
6. Kansas	53.3	18. N. Y.	49.2	30. R. I.	44.8	42. N. C.	34.6
7. N. D.	53.3	19. Wis.	49.1	31. Colo.	44.8	43. Ky.	33.6
8. Ohio	53.0	20. Utah	49.0	32. Penn.	44.6	44. Ala.	32.4
9. Mich.	52.6	21. S. D.	48.8	33. Md.	44.1	45. Tenn.	31.6
10. Idaho	52.1	22. Ore.	48.7	34. La.	43.9	46. Ark.	31.1
11. N. H.	51.8	23. Minn.	48.4	35. Mo.	43.8	47. Ga.	30.8
12. Mont.	50.9	24. Conn.	48.2	36. Mass.	43.8	48. Va.	29.9

eight states in the union prior to 1888, the ten with highest ratios were, in order: California, Kansas, Ohio, Michigan, New Hampshire, West Virginia, Iowa, New Jersey, Indiana, and New York. The lowest of the late arrivals—South Dakota—was twenty-first in the rankings, which means that all nine of these new western states were in the upper 43 per cent of the states. Twelve of the first twenty-two states were western.

The lowest quartile has nine southern states, two Border states (Delaware and Kentucky), and Maine of the East. The unflinching Democracy of all but Maine accounts for their ineffectiveness. Maine, Massachusetts, and Pennsylvania are consistent Republican states, with large Democratic minorities. Thus, all votes were lost in years of Democratic victory and large minorities were ineffective in the Republican years. The ratio of ineffectiveness for many southern states was reduced by two factors. In the years of political drought for that section, the total vote dwindled; with Franklin D. Roosevelt, the southern vote leaped to new highs. In fact, from 1904 to 1936, the southern vote increased 268.9 per cent. Over one-half of that increase has come in the last three elections, two of which were Democratic landslides.

In general, the states of strong opposition parties, in contrast to third party states, are in the second and third quartiles. The leading third-party states are in the first, but in these the Democratic party, with the exception of Ohio and New Hampshire, has not been consistent in its strength.

Voter Participation

The test of any party system in a democracy is the degree

GEOGRAPHY OF DECISION

to which it interests the great body of citizenry in public questions. The greater the number participating the more democratic the system. The question of whether popular decisions are preferable to those derived from other sources is not germane to this discussion. The United States is jealous of its democratic tradition, and any other system is— and for a hundred years has been so regarded—outside the realm of possibility. But how democratic is this system?

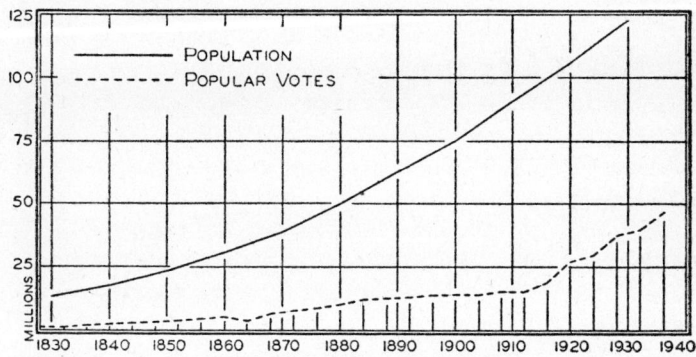

Figure 8.—Population and Popular Votes

Much learned writing has been done upon the undemocratic bases of the early United States government, about the anti-democratic factors and personnel in the Constitutional Convention of 1787, and about the wholesale discrimination practiced against classes and races in this country up until the beginning of the period under discussion here. The present study leaves that earlier period to the historians and moves into post-Civil-War America for its investigational excursions.

In *Figure 8*, the population and popular-vote trends are shown. To reveal the basic trends more effectively, the graph includes the population figures from 1830 to 1930 and the vote statistics from 1828 to 1936. If the population had increased no faster after the Civil War than from 1830 to 1860, the 1930 population would have been little in excess of ninety millions. But, after 1870, the ascending line became more precipitous. The interesting point in the graph is that the total-vote line, except for the reduction in the war election of 1864, runs a relatively even course from 1828 to 1912. Thereafter the line, by fits and starts, rises at almost the same degree as the population line. One obvious interpretation of this belated electoral increase is that women were enumerated as people by the census takers but were not, except in a few states, (for the most part sparsely-settled western ones) permitted to exercise the franchise. In only twelve states, the most populous being Illinois and California, were women entitled to vote for presidential electors in 1916.[3]

There was a more important factor than the denial of the franchise to women in the failure of the vote line to ascend at a more acute angle. The population grew from 26,045,006 in 1880 to 54,908,425 in 1908, yet the total popular votes of those two years were, respectively, 9,207,936 and 14,887,133. Thus, in this twenty-eight-year span, the population in-

[3] The woman-suffrage states, and the years in which the franchise was extended, were: Wyoming (statehood, 1890), Colorado (1893), Utah and Idaho (1896), Washington (1910), California (1911), Arizona, Kansas, and Oregon (1912), Montana and Nevada (1914) and Illinois, for presidential electors (1913). Four other states—New York (1917) and Michigan, Oklahoma, and South Dakota (1918)—granted the franchise to women before the Nineteenth Amendment extended it to all states in 1920. However, as no presidential election occurred during that interim, the fact that these were also woman-suffrage states before 1920 is of only academic importance.

GEOGRAPHY OF DECISION

creased 110.8 per cent and the total vote only 61.7 per cent. There was, therefore, a tremendous lag in the exercise of the franchise. Of course, the restrictive measures in the South accounted for some of the slack, but only a small portion of it. This was the period in which the new industrial order was being developed. Presumably, when a people is busily engaged in the creation of vital economic institutions, there is little time for politics.

These were the years of genuine political cynicism in America. The popular literature exalted the traditional American virtues of frugality, individual initiative, and respect for hard work. Politicians were caricatured as ne'er-do-wells, who were totally nonconversant with the dynamic principles of the new order. There were higher truths which, according to the gospel of success, were denied to the uninitiate. This was the new occultism. To become rich was somehow the most important desideratum. Poets, professors, and *literati* became the jesters of the new age. They sang their lyrics in the palaces of the *nouveau riche*. Anyone who challenged the moral values of financial civilization was branded a "socialist," an "anarchist," or a "muckraker."

The revolt against this new order flared on the plains of the great American hinterland. The Populists threatened the hegemony of the financial barons, but "Mark" Hanna beat them down in 1896 with the largest campaign fund that had ever been raised in this country. However, the cry for intervention welled up even in the ranks of those who had fallen victim to the propaganda of Hanna's hired hands and even a Republican president was forced to move against the concentration of economic power. "Trust-busting" was popular with the common people, and when the Republicans refused to carry on the reform program, party schism and Democratic national triumph were the immediate results.

The demand for governmental intervention arose in the analysis of social effects that derived in unrestrained industrialism. When these social questions were brought into political campaigns, an increasing number of persons had vital interest in the outcome of elections. This accounts for much of the phenomenal recent increase in the popular canvass—from twenty-nine to forty-five millions from 1924 to 1936. And there may be anticipated even greater increases in the future if these social questions remain paramount in American politics.

In 1860, the most critical year in all American electoral history, an average of but 148.7 of every one thousand persons in the national population participated in the general election. That is, roughly, a one-to-seven ratio. In 1936, for every one thousand persons, 336 ballots were cast. Thus in seventy-six years the American people have moved from a one-to-seven to a one-to-three proportion. The data for the twenty elections are shown in TABLE 21.

In the table, two bases—adults (people over twenty years of age)[4] and total population—are employed to present the fundamental trends of the electoral system. Beginning with 1860, the electorate was augmented in two directions—both by increased population and by an extension of voting privileges. However, the latter was far less important than the

[4] The data for the adult portions of the national population were assembled from Warren S. Thompson and P. K. Whelpton, *Population Trends in the United States* (New York: McGraw-Hill, 1933), x, 415. As the data here given were only for census years, the figure for each national election that did not fall in a census year is based upon the presumption that the increase in the number of adults within a decennial period was one of regular arithmetical progression.

GEOGRAPHY OF DECISION

former in increasing the ballot count, for the increase in ratio of adults who voted was but 80 per cent, while that in ratio of the entire population was 126 per cent. The difference lies in the increasing percentage of adults in the whole population; for, while the population increase from 1860 to 1930 was 290.5 per cent, the corresponding increase in persons over twenty years of age was 440 per cent. Thus, if the same ratio of adults had voted in 1936 as voted in 1860, the total popular vote would have been 25,183,553 as against the 45,402,849

TABLE 21.—POPULAR VOTES PER THOUSAND POPULATION, 1860-1936

Year	All people	Adults	Year	All people	Adults
1860	148.7	306.1	1900	186.0	329.6
1864	161.3		1904	166.0	287.2
1868	155.9	308.1	1908	167.6	289.1
1872	160.5	312.3	1912	156.9	272.8
1876	187.6	359.4	1916	183.5	311.6
1880	186.3	353.4	1920	253.5	426.8
1884	194.7	360.6	1924	259.4	430.6
1888	194.3	353.4	1928	309.6	507.3
1892	184.1	340.5	1932	314.0	512.1
1896	197.7	355.5	1936	336.0	549.7

ballots actually cast in that year. On the other hand, if the population of 1936 had had the same ratio of adults as that of 1860, there would have been but 65,759,000 adults in the forty-eight states as against the 82,599,000 who were actually there. And if these hypothetical sixty-five million adults had voted in the same proportion in 1936 as their forbears did in 1860, the total vote in the last election would have been but 20,128,992 in contrast to the more than forty-five million. This shows the dominating influence which the increase in

PRESIDENTIAL ELECTIONS

the total population's adult percentage has had upon the increase in the total popular vote.

The sectional records of voter participation, constructed from the basis of the number of votes per thousand inhabitants, are shown in *Figure 9*. The most striking generaliza-

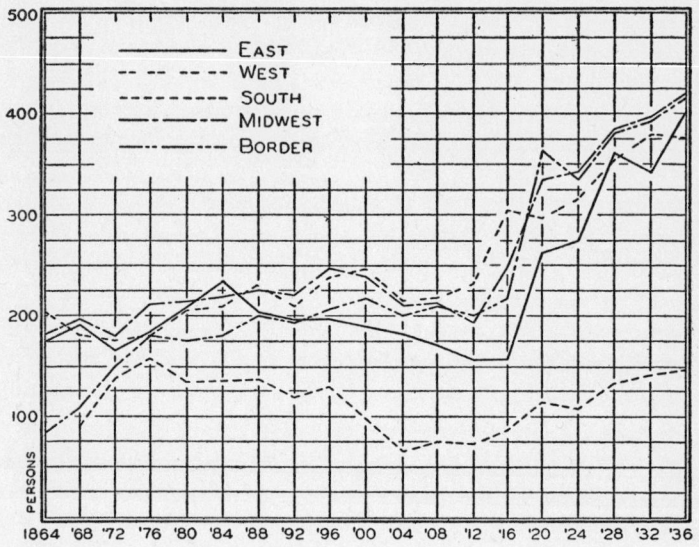

Figure 9.—Votes per Thousand Inhabitants: by Sections

tion to be drawn from the graph is that the South is a section apart from the implementation of the democratic process in the United States. Even during the controversial Reconstruction period, this section showed the smallest percentage of voter participation, and thereafter the record becomes steadily worse. Many have engaged in prolix apologia, promising improvement in the years to come. Whatever the potentialities may be for extension of the franchise in the South, one may conclude that, as yet, their realization is not discernible from the ballot statistics, and that the trends are still far behind those of other sections. In other words, the South, from the point of view of the democratic process, is falling far behind the rest of the United States.

The large Negro population in the section is the central point of almost every southern argument. But this thorny problem, whatever its merits, is of minor significance as compared with the more fundamental one of southern psychology. If one assumes that there had been no increase in Negro population after 1930,[5] there were more than eight and one-half million Negroes of all ages in the twelve southern states in 1932. Thus, there were approximately twenty-three and one-half million whites in those states. Even if no southern Negro cast a ballot in 1932, the ratio of voter participation in that section was but 190.5 per thousand white inhabitants, or about the average for the other four sections in the immediate post-Civil-War era and only 47.5 per cent of the average in the other four sections in 1936. The great impediment to the achievement of popular participation in politics in the South lies in the traditions of the section. In reality, the franchise there has the old familiar Hellenistic basis. This is not, of course, precisely accurate, but it is generally true of the section. The poll tax and cumulative poll tax requirements, the understanding clauses, and the white primary exclusions stand as stark proof of the general relevancy of this generalization.

Democracy implies faith in the public decisions of citi-

[5] See graph in Thompson and Whelpton, *op. cit.*, 9.

zens. When the ruling classes convince themselves that people cannot be trusted, there is no hope for the successful operation of democracy. The defenders of fascist régimes mouth these same arguments about the "fool public." It must be admitted that democratic decisions are many times at variance with philosophic truth, but the fact remains that democracy implies popular participation in politics and that today, when compulsory attendance has for many decades been the basis of our public school systems, the general citizenry should be more capable of rendering public decisions than ever before. If the latter proposition is not true, then great sums of money may well be saved to the taxpayers.

There are many who maintain that the certainty of Democratic triumph reduces the number of voters in the South. One must admit the accuracy of this observation. It would be doubly true but for the legal disfranchisement. When laws are passed to restrict the franchise, the voluntary non-voting problem is of lesser moment. The mere failure to vote is never a threat to democratic society. In a country of free elections, the smaller poll would certainly tend to show that the existing government was performing its functions in an approved manner. And when the vote increased, there would be evidence that that approval was not so universal. Therefore, the mere fact that the South has a small poll is not so deprecatory as the will to keep it small is. Thus, as is shown in the graph (*Figure* 9), the South presents problem number one of American democracy. The result of the widespread restriction of the franchise is to deter the formation of an opposition party in the South. Thus, for sixty years, the section has been turning in a vicious circle of a shamefully small electorate and a one-party system. If either of these two phenomena were to be abolished, the other would pass, and the section might develop a democratic order like that of the other sections.

In the period from 1868 to 1876, each of the eleven southern states had a participation ratio of more than one hundred voters per thousand inhabitants, and seven of them were above one hundred fifty. Though not so high as that of the Middle West, this was a very respectable record. During the next four elections, three states—South Carolina, Georgia, and Mississippi—slipped under the hundred mark. For the third period, even though the great Bryan campaigns occurred in it, only North Carolina, Tennessee, and Oklahoma remained above. Of the other nine, Mississippi and South Carolina sank to new lows—40.2 and 41.9 per thousand, respectively. Even with woman suffrage, four states—South Carolina, Georgia, Alabama, and Mississippi—still linger beneath the hundred mark, with South Carolina's 46.9 per thousand at the bottom. However, Oklahoma and North Carolina each had a participation ratio above two hundred.

Of the other four sections, there are few observations that need be made. The Border was behind the other three sections before 1892, but since that time it has maintained the pace, and in 1916, it was highest in the nation. The East presents a curious record. Though having been above the two-hundred mark in the three elections immediately preceding, in 1892 the section's poll fell below that mark and for six elections it went steadily downward until it stood just above 140 in each of the 1912 and the 1916 contests. Woman suffrage took it upward eighty points in 1920.

There are several factors to be considered in the decline

of the East. This was a period of intense European immigration into that area. Millions of adult Europeans entered the American population. Most were inexperienced in the American way of deciding political issues, and many had never cast a ballot in their lives. Another factor was the reduction in popularity as a result of the fusion of the Democratic party and the "radical" Populists. The section's Democratic polls dwindled, and with them the section's record in voter participation. A final factor is that of industrial organization. These were the years when the East's industrial order was reaching its maturity. The labor movement was still in its infancy, not yet ready to challenge the factory owners in the field of politics. These were the years when people glibly relied upon economic progress to salve whatever political ills they had, years in which men hoped for business in government rather than government in business. It was a period of political skepticism, of rising wages (both money and real), and of increasing industrial expansion! Democracy, as it is known today, may yet prove workable only among dominantly agrarian people.

The Middle West and West, both agrarian, have since 1864 led all sections, except for two elections. Theirs is an independent people, who come to the polls to protest or to approve. These citizens were not deterred in their right to vote their convictions as were the industrial workers of the East and the poorer classes—both white and black—of the South. A contemporary de Tocqueville would have to observe that there, west of the Alleghenies and north of the Ohio lies a tremendous stretch of territory, inhabited by more than fifty million people who have been trained from birth in the best traditions of a free, democratic society,

GEOGRAPHY OF DECISION

wherein the registering of conviction, whether approval or protest, is the respected right of every citizen regardless of race, color, or economic status.[6]

To consider the averages of several states as descriptive of the entire section does injustice to the individual states. Oklahoma is a case in point, for its participation record is almost four times that of the South's cellar states, and almost twice that of the section's average. TABLE 22 contains the participation averages of each state for the four subdivisions and for the entire period. A close scrutiny of the upper quartiles for the five temporal periods shows that twenty-two states have on one or more occasions been members of that select group. Indiana and Nevada have been there in every period, while New Hampshire, Ohio, Wyoming, Colorado, and Kansas have three periods to their credit. Those with two are Oregon, California, Michigan, Montana, Washington, and Illinois.[7]

The introduction of woman suffrage into twelve states before the adoption of the Nineteenth Amendment serves to disrupt the relative value of these statistics. Ten of the upper quartile states in the third period were woman-suffrage states. Naturally, they would rise to that high place, though a similar status would not have lifted any southern state, with the possible exception of Oklahoma, into the charmed group. The high places of Indiana, Ohio, and Iowa are all the more remarkable, since they earned their records with only manhood suffrage.

[6] It is not meant to infer that states like Missouri and Oklahoma have placed great impediments in the path of voter participation, yet the spirit, for instance, of these two states is not so democratic as that of their common neighbor, Kansas. There have been vast differences between Kentucky and Indiana or Ohio, and between Tennessee and Illinois.

[7] The one-period states are Connecticut, New York, Utah, Idaho, Delaware, Missouri, Iowa, West Virginia, and Nebraska.

PRESIDENTIAL ELECTIONS

TABLE 22.—VOTER PARTICIPATION PER THOUSAND INHABITANTS: BY STATE AND PERIOD

1864-1876			State	Rank	Ratio	State	Rank	Ratio
			Tenn.	35	122.2	Vt.	29	183.8
State	Rank	Ratio	Tex.	36	117.9	N. C.	30	175.3
			R. I.	37	90.9	Va.	31	170.9
Nev.	1	397.1				Ky.	32	170.7
Ore.	2	226.0				N. D.	33	164.4
N. H.	3	220.8	1880-1892					
Ind.	4	210.8				Mass.	34	160.1
Ohio	5	201.1				Tenn.	35	158.9
Cal.	6	198.7	State	Rank	Ratio	Fla.	36	155.6
Mich.	7	196.0				Tex.	37	148.1
Conn.	8	192.1	Mont.	1	271.8	Ark.	38	135.5
N. Y.	9	190.4	Wyo.*	2	243.7	Ala.	39	125.1
			Ind.	3	243.3	R. I.	40	122.4
N. J.	10	188.2	Nev.	4	243.2	La.	41	105.8
Wis.	11	188.1	N. H.	5	240.5	Ga.	42	96.5
Fla.	12	181.4	Colo.	6	236.9	S. C.	43	94.6
Minn.	13	181.4	Ohio	7	229.7	Miss.	44	82.5
Pa.	14	179.1	Ore.	8	226.4			
Iowa	15	176.6	Kans.	9	225.7			
Vt.	16	175.2	Wash.	10	225.4	1896-1916			
Ill.	17	170.4	Mich.	11	217.2			
Me.	18	168.7						
			N. Y.	12	217.1	State	Rank	Ratio
N. C.	19	167.6	N. J.	13	216.0			
La.	20	165.4	Iowa	14	214.8	Colo.*	1	356.1
S. C.	21	164.6	Wis.	15	212.5	Utah*	2	319.3
Kans.	22	164.4	Conn.	16	210.4	Idaho*	3	319.0
Del.	23	161.1	Ill.	17	206.0	Kans.*	4	304.7
Va.	24	156.8	Cal.	18	205.6	Nev.*	5	290.0
Miss.	25	155.0	W. Va.	19	203.6	Wyo.*	6	275.2
Neb.	26	154.3	Neb.	20	198.6	Ind.	7	256.9
Ala.	27	152.8	Del.	21	198.2	Mont.*	8	254.8
			Me.	22	197.2	Ill.*	9	243.8
Md.	28	146.5				Cal.*	10	237.0
Mass.	29	139.4	S. D.	23	196.3	Wash.*	11	233.7
Mo.	30	131.0	Md.	24	195.5	Ohio	12	231.2
Ky.	31	129.0	Pa.	25	193.3			
W. Va.	32	128.7	Mo.	26	192.3	Ore.*	13	230.7
Ark.	33	128.1	Minn.	27	190.9	Iowa	14	226.9
Ga.	34	126.7	Idaho	28	190.0	Del.	15	225.5

* Woman-suffrage state.

TABLE 22.—Voter Participation per Thousand Inhabitants: by State and Period (*Continued*)

State	Rank	Ratio	State	Rank	Ratio	State	Rank	Ratio
W. Va.	16	218.8	Ga.	45	53.7	Ky.	20	354.6
S. D.	17	216.0	La.	46	51.2	R. I.	21	352.7
Neb.	18	213.3	S. C.	47	41.9	Ore.	22	349.8
Mo.	19	212.2	Miss.	48	40.2	N. D.	23	348.4
N. H.	20	210.3				Wash.	24	343.4
Ky.	21	209.4						
Mich.	22	204.5	1920–1936			N. Y.	25	342.2
Wis.	23	196.6				Mass.	26	340.5
Md.	24	194.7				Vt.	27	339.9
			State	Rank	Ratio	Wis.	28	337.2
N. Y.	25	188.1				Cal.	29	329.2
N. J.	26	187.4	Del.	1	452.0	Conn.	30	325.6
N. M.	27	173.6	Ind.	2	449.9	Md.	31	325.1
Conn.	28	173.3	Mo.	3	422.7	N. M.	32	317.8
Pa.	29	172.5	N. H.	4	409.6	Maine	33	314.6
Minn.	30	170.3	Ia.	5	408.1	Mich.	34	301.9
N. D.	31	168.3	Ill.	6	403.9	Pa.	35	298.7
Vt.	32	166.4	Kans.	7	398.3	Okla.	36	264.6
Ariz.*	33	158.9	W. Va.	8	393.2			
Me.	34	154.3	Nev.	9	387.7	Ariz.	37	220.2
Okla.	35	152.2	Colo.	10	385.1	N. C.	38	204.7
Mass.	36	144.8	Neb.	11	380.2	Fla.	39	158.0
			Wyo.	12	379.2	Tenn.	40	153.7
R. I.	37	139.4				Tex.	41	126.2
N. C.	38	129.0	Ohio	13	374.8	Va.	42	115.9
Tenn.	39	127.4	Idaho	14	372.9	La.	43	103.6
Tex.	40	99.2	Minn.	15	367.9	Ark.	44	100.3
Va.	41	95.7	Utah	16	362.6	Ala.	45	90.1
Ark.	42	93.8	Mont.	17	362.0	Ga.	46	68.5
Fla.	43	74.7	S. D.	18	361.4	Miss.	47	66.5
Ala.	44	66.4	N. J.	19	357.9	S. C.	48	46.9

If the woman-suffrage states be excluded from the third-period rankings, the upper quartile would be composed of Indiana, Ohio, Iowa, Delaware, West Virginia, South Dakota, Nebraska, Missouri, and New Hampshire. Thus, all sections except the South would be represented, with the Middle West and Border having three places, the West two, and the East one. However, several of these woman-suffrage states had very respectable participation records before woman suffrage. This was especially true of Washington, Kansas, Nevada, and Oregon. To exclude them with the excuse that their high places were the result of the enfranchisement of women would be distinctly unfair. Six of them were in the upper quartile for the second period.

The increase in the votes of these twelve states cannot be accurately determined. However, the nine states which adopted the reform after having participated in presidential elections show an average increase of 40.1 per cent for the first woman-suffrage elections. Of course, some of this increase would have come without women's votes, but there exists no way to determine its dimensions. Moreover, in seven of the nine states, the poll in the election before women voted for the first time showed a loss over the immediately preceding one. Since all of these losses were achieved in either 1892 or 1912, when the rate of participation fell off generally throughout the country, one must assume that women accounted for much less of the increase than the 40 per cent. In Indiana, without woman suffrage the 1916 increase was 9.1 per cent, in Kentucky 15 per cent, and in Maine it was 27 per cent.

The reactions of the sections to the implementation of the Nineteenth Amendment were varied. In the South, the participation ratio was slow to rise after 1920. Though other factors intervened to increase the citizens' interest in politics, the difference between the participation ratios of the third and fourth periods will throw some light upon the effect of woman suffrage. The increases in the sections were: East (87.6 per cent), Border (81.6 per cent), Middle West (68.2

per cent), South (46.7 per cent), and West (42.3 per cent). The low rate of the West resulted from the fact that eleven of the fifteen states permitted women to vote before 1920. For the other four states, the average increase was 82.5 per cent. On the other hand, Colorado, with woman suffrage throughout the last two periods, has an increase in participation of 8.1 per cent for the last period, and Wyoming, always a woman-suffrage state, shows an increase of 38.5 per cent over its third-period mark.

The participation rate of the South was slow in showing an appreciable rise after the adoption of the amendment. Even in 1924, the average rate for the South was but 17.9 per cent above that for the third period. South Carolina, Georgia, Alabama, Florida, Mississippi, Louisiana, Arkansas, and Virginia are still below their high participation marks of the Reconstruction period. North Carolina and Tennessee did not pass theirs until 1920, and Texas not until 1924. In South Carolina, the nadir was reached after woman suffrage, for only 29.8 persons per thousand voted in 1924. This figure was but 14.3 per cent of the state's high mark of 1876. Mississippi's low of 34.5 was but 21.2 per cent of her 1876 high.

The anomalous position of the South is more graphically depicted in *Figure 10*. Here the base is the average voter participation in the whole United States, and the graph lines show each section's relation to that average base in each of the nineteen elections. The South has never reached the nation's average, though it was reasonably close to it in 1872 and 1876. Thereafter, the Democratic hegemony, with its informal as well as formal techniques for protection of that régime through franchise restrictions, steered a steadily descending course until 1904, when it dropped below the 40 per cent mark. Since then, it has hovered just above that level. To the apology that the franchise conditions are improving in the South, this graph offers an emphatic "no."

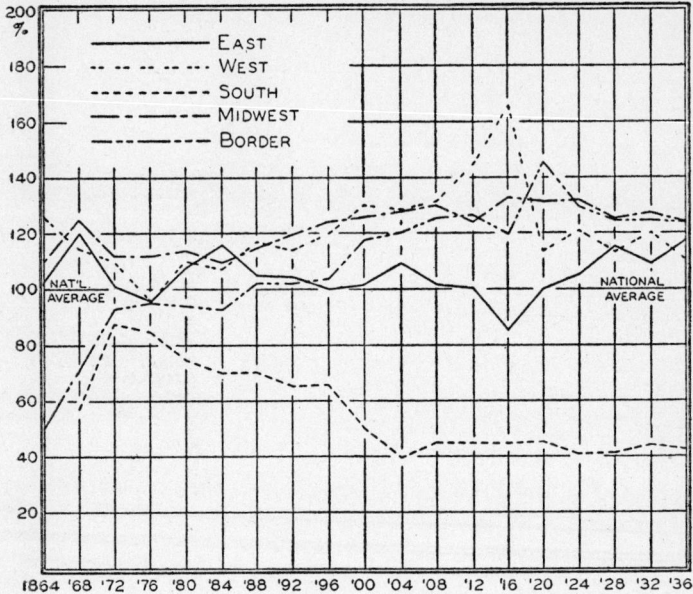

Figure 10.—Sectional Percentages of Average National Voter Participation

For that section, in relation to the entire nation, is now in even worse position than in 1908.

The Border was below the national average in the first six elections, but it has, since 1888, taken its place among the other sections that hold no fear of large popular participa-

GEOGRAPHY OF DECISION

tion. The East has been the "average section." In two elections, it was below the national average; in eight it was very near the 100 per cent line; in the other nine it was above, with peaks of 120 per cent being reached in 1868 and 1936. Though the West was below the standard in 1876, it was well above in the other eighteen, with its 1916 poll setting a record of 165 per cent. However, it must be remembered that this high mark may be attributed in part to woman suffrage. The Middle West was the banner section, being not only above the national average in every election but far above it in most. In twelve of the nineteen contests, this section's mark was above 120 per cent. Here, then, has abided, continuously since the Civil War, American democracy in its finest tradition.

After 1920, the graph lines for the upper four sections draw generally to a common point, from which one could conclude that the franchise in this country is finally achieving a national, rather than a mere sectional, aspect. The South, of course is not included in this generalization.

One more correlation remains to be made. One who is interested in the dynamics of the democratic process should determine the average number of effective votes per thousand residents for each of the nineteen elections. A fair index of this phenomenon may be secured by multiplying the percentage of effectiveness by the participation ratio for each state. The results are shown in TABLE 23.

The rate of effectiveness per thousand inhabitants ranged from 22.8 in Georgia to 180.5 in Idaho. Thus, from 1868 to 1936, only 2.28 per cent of Georgia citizens, per election, cast their ballots for winning electors of the triumphant national party. Only Oklahoma, of the twelve Southern states, had an average exceeding 10 per cent. The upper quartile was monopolized by the West and Middle West, ten to two, but six of these ten were newer states, and nine permitted women to vote before 1920. The second group of twelve states comprises three eastern, one Border, three middle western, and five western states. Thus all western states were in the upper one-half of states. The third group

TABLE 23.—AVERAGE EFFECTIVE POPULAR VOTES PER THOUSAND INHABITANTS: BY STATES, 1864-1936

Upper Quartile			Second Quartile			Third Quartile			Lower Quartile		
State	Rank	Ratio	State	Rank	Ratio	State	Rank	Ratio	State	Rank	Ratio
Idaho	1	180.5	N. H.	13	144.2	Minn.	25	124.5	Ky.	37	80.4
Wyo.	2	180.0	W. Va.	14	142.9	Wis.	26	123.4	Fla.	38	60.3
Utah	3	168.2	Ill.	15	141.4	Conn.	27	117.6	N. C.	39	57.5
Kan.	4	165.4	N. D.	16	140.9	Mo.	28	117.6	Tex.	40	44.5
Cal.	5	162.9	Ore.	17	140.5	Okla.	29	114.7	Tenn.	41	43.4
Wash.	6	160.4	Iowa	18	140.3	Del.	30	112.1	La.	42	38.9
N. M.	7	159.8	S. D.	19	139.4	Vt.	31	104.3	Va.	43	34.1
Mont.	8	159.4	N. J.	20	133.2	Md.	32	100.4	Ark.	44	31.2
Colo.	9	157.3	Mich.	21	131.1	Pa.	33	100.3	Ala.	45	29.4
Ind.	10	154.1	Neb.	22	130.4	Mass.	34	97.5	S. C.	46	27.4
Nev.	11	151.3	Ariz.	23	127.0	R. I.	35	97.4	Miss.	47	24.2
Ohio	12	149.5	N. Y.	24	125.2	Me.	36	89.9	Ga.	48	22.8

had six eastern, three Border, two middle western, and one southern state. The lowest quartile comprised eleven southern states and Kentucky, a Border state. The average rank of the West was 15.5, of the Middle West 18.1, the East 28.1, the Border 28.2, and the South 41.7. This reveals better than rhetoric the effectiveness of the various sections in the making of political decisions in America.

GEOGRAPHY OF DECISION

Summary

From the preceding discussion there emerges a picture of American politics, the outlines of which are not clear if too close scrutiny is given to the political behavior of particular states. The Reconstruction era witnessed the union of the East and Middle West upon the issues that surrounded the war between the states. When the Democrats returned to power in the South, they sought to stand upon their traditional ground of states' rights, little realizing that the national effectiveness of that doctrine passed with the failure of the great John C. Calhoun to stem the drive against the institution of human slavery.

After 1892, the Democrats became the champions of human, as against property, rights, but they experienced difficulty in securing the union of any sections with the South upon an enduring basis. The American people, not unlike the people of any other national state, prefer prosperous economic conditions and were slow to support the party that was in power during the depression of the middle nineties. "Democrats are bad for business" became an accepted truism in the East and Middle West. Likewise, after the turn of the century, the Republicans undertook the task of compromising the differences between industrialism and agrarianism, thus making the rôle of the Democrats more difficult than it might otherwise have been. For if the Republicans had reflected the interests of one to the economic detriment of the other, the Democrats might have entrenched themselves in sections other than the South.

When the Republicans were unable to satisfy agrarians of

the equity of the platform compromises, the Democrats came to power as the party of governmental intervention. For when business leaders objected to government in business and workers and farmers relied upon it, there came a division in American politics that could scarcely be compromised by a single party. The Democrats were slow to see their opportunity in the late twenties. Too much of the party leadership was from the South, a section that still looked with disfavor upon the regulation of individuals by the central government.

The vote and participation charts reveal the fundamental change in American political habits in the days of Democratic-Populist fusion. A new political order was born in those stormy years. No party could hope for electoral success through reliance upon the nineteenth century principles of *laissez faire*. The Republicans fought off the threat of Bryanism and surrendered in part to its principles.

The problems that arose in the industrial system and in its clash with the remaining agrarian interests contributed the issues for American politics after 1896. More and more people came to have personal interests in these problems. The vote totals and the participation ratios rose. The country now stands at the peak for its entire history, but increased vote totals are still in prospect. American people have called their system democratic throughout their history, and in that they were no doubt correct. But the differences between the Andrew Jackson democratic *milieu* and that of Franklin Delano Roosevelt are very pronounced.

CHAPTER SIX

An Interpretation

THE graphs and tables of this study present a picture of American politics, which, without the color and personalities of individual campaigns, is as monochromatic as a statistical summary. But the personal pyrotechnics of campaigns are only a means to an end, a technique employed to influence the decisions of perplexed voters. The real story of American politics lies in the slow mutation of the political mores of the whole people. Economic conditions may, in this day of hair-trigger systems, cry for immediate solutions, but public thought, moored safely and securely to the experience of the past, will scarcely ever leap forward with a ready formula. At best, there will be a long period of indecision, characterized by a decreased ratio of voter participation, after which a sufficient number of voters will finally come to support a common remedy.

The wheels of democratic progress grind at a painfully slow pace, but they nonetheless grind, and they are difficult to throw out of alignment. Most of the time, the intellectual, impatient with popular indecision in a period of crisis, fails to appreciate the travail of public decision. Democracies come frequently to the cross roads. Though appearing to fumble, they ultimately make their choice; and a people usually has an uncanny sense of direction. Learned men today emphasize the indispensability of planned economy and the people listen and try to reconcile the proposals with the traditional doctrines of competitive economics. When the decision, for or against, may be given is a subject for conjecture. Presumably many half-way stations will be tested before it is forthcoming.

It must be remembered that the solution of the slavery issue was a long time in coming, and indeed only at a tremendous cost. Black men were born in an era in which liberation was being talked. They lived their whole lives as slaves and died before the assault upon Fort Sumter. Many leaders of that crusade had long since abandoned hope of its realization before the public conviction made further postponement of a settlement a difficult, if not impossible, political compromise.

As the period under discussion opened, the sections were locked in mortal combat. The South lost, but the democratic convictions that had ripened in the preceding decades were sufficient to prevent the introduction of new political issues for almost a quarter of a century. "Political freeedom" was the perfumed phrase of the hour and the battles of the war were re-fought upon the political platforms of both sections until the rise of the Populist party shifted attention to a new threat to individual freedom—the threat of the money power. A new Jacksonian era was born! Epithets that once were rained on Nicholas Biddle and his bank were, sixty years later, resuscitated for the agrarian's abomination of Wall Street.

Through the seventies and the eighties crusaders speculated upon the content of liberty. Third parties sprang up like mushrooms in the farflung agricultural regions of the

AN INTERPRETATION

nation. Specific panaceas were of minor importance, but they succeeded one another with surprising spirit; always behind them was the desire for an economic substance for political liberty. Finally, by 1890, a million men had agreed that the government should intervene to protect private citizens. In 1892, Grover Cleveland was elected upon a nineteenth century platform of non-interference. Four years later, the Democratic program was one of full fledged interventionism. Here was a modern program, the product of public thinking over a period of a quarter-century.

The Republicans, the traditional party, appealed to the experience of the people and, for the nonce, the people were fearful of their own thinking. They could not believe that they wanted the government to play so prominent a rôle in the affairs of men. They hesitated at the choice and tradition triumphed over mind. However, in less than a decade, the Republicans were the victims of the virus which they sought to destroy in 1896. They had won a battle only to lose a campaign. And thereafter no political party could successfully appeal upon a non-interventionist platform. The last three decades, rudely jolted by the war effort, have witnessed the attempt to determine what degree of intervention will best conduce to individual integrity upon one hand and collective efficiency upon the other.

There is another important facet to American political history. This is the influence which sectional coalitions have had upon national politics. The war between the states was essentially a union of the East and Middle West against the South. For thirty years that coalition was held together by war memories and traditions. Without realizing that the political effectiveness of the states' rights doctrine had passed in John C. Calhoun's abortive attempt to protect southern institutions with it, the Democrats clung to it as a drowning man clutches a straw. To the citizens of the East and Middle West, states' rights were synonymous to the desire to destroy the Union. The idea was antithetical to the new nationalism that developed after Appomattox.

As electoral stimuli, the war memories dimmed in the late eighties and early nineties, but the stake of the two dominant sections in the industrial empire was sufficient to retain the coalition intact. The South was again on the losing political side, though it received spotted support from both the Border and the West. Though more important earlier, the sixteen states of the East and Middle West today lack only three electoral votes of having a majority in the electoral college. Thus, when these two dominant industrial sections present a solid political front they are almost assured a national victory.

Even in the present transitional stage, there exist strong evidences that the great hinterland and the larger industrial states of the East may become the ruling sections of America. When the crisis came in the industrial organization, the South might have taken the lead in the formation of a new sectional coalition. But its conscious martyrdom and its suffrage restrictions have apparently destroyed that possibility. The section is as yet outside the main stream of American political thinking. If it were to let down the bars to political participation it might become again, after an absence of a hundred years, a part of the organic American political public. The extension of industrial enterprise in the South is a strong factor in that realization, for the section must consequently face problems that are common to the remainder of the United States.

INDEX

Index

★ ★ ★ ★ ★ ★ ★ ★

Abolitionism, strength in Middle West, 72, 73
Adult participation, decline of, 14
Agrarian democracy, reaction to corporate industrialism, 25, 26; view of "colonial" sections, 46; in the South, 62, 63; in Middle West, 72, 73
Agrarian parties, in the East, 112, 113; votes in sections, 113; in Border, 114; in South, 114, 115; in West, 116, 117
Agricultural economy, small holding in Border, 10
Agriculture, passing of frontier, 6; crisis in, 36, 37; influence of in West, 89, 90
America, and democracy abroad, 33, 34
Annual Cyclopaedia, 13
Anti-alienism, in early twenties, 33, 34
Anti-monopoly party, 26
Anti-Saloon League, 132
Arthur, Chester A., 23
"Artificial Decade," 34; Republican success in East during, 52, 53
Ashby, "Stump," 26

Beecher, Henry Ward, 23
Bellamy, 6
Beveridge, Albert J., 79
Biddle, Nicholas, 216
Bingham, Barry, 68
Borah, William E., 98
Border, defined, 10; and Reconstruction, 10; heritage from *ante bellum* period, 56, 57; on preservation of Union, 57, 58; votes in 1860, 57n.; anti-Republican, 58, 59; effect of 1896 election on voter allegiance, 58-62; and agrarian parties, 114; and Prohibition party, 118, 119; in electoral college, 147, 148, 150; five-per-cent elections, 153, 154; effectiveness in electoral college, 173; wastage of popular votes, 178, 181; voter participation in, 203
Bryan, W. J., campaign of 1896, 12; and fusion, 28; third race, 30; popularity in Middle West, 75; third race and Middle West, 78; and Spanish American War, 94; third race, in West, 95, 98

Calhoun, John C., 217
Catholicism, unpopularity of in South (Smith campaign), 69-71
Christensen, 98; 116
Civil War, in United States history, 1, 3; cost, 5; memories of, 5; influence on politics of Middle West, 12; and Democratic respectability, 14; influence of on political allegiance, 18; and Middle West, 72, 73
Clay, Henry, defeat in 1844, 133, 134
Cleveland, Grover, reform candidate,

PRESIDENTIAL ELECTIONS

23; attitude of West toward, 91; popular vote in 1888, 137

Constitution, 1; and slavocracy, 3; a human document, 4; ideas behind, 42, 43

Coolidge, Calvin, 34; 35; 37; and economic imbalance, 39; 82

Cooper, Peter, 13

Corporate industrialism, reaction to in Border, 60-62

Corporations, railroad, in politics, 5

Cotton, 3

Cox, James, 34; middle western reaction to, 82; 98

Cummins, Albert B., 30, 79

Curtis, vii

Curtis, Francis, 13; cited, 22

Curtis, George William, 23

Dangerfield, R. J., viii

Davis, "Cyclone," 26

Davis, John W., 35; unpopularity in West, 99

Debs, 98

Delaware, 10

Democracy, agrarian, 2; individualistic, 2; equalitarian, 4; slowness of process, 215-17

Democratic party, loss of dominance, 4; and liberty, 8; national triumphs, 14; rise in prestige in East, 54; 1892 crisis in South, 67, 68; 1904 loss in Middle West, 76-79; rise in Middle West after 1920, 84-86; in Middle West, 86, 87; state percentages of popular votes, 105, 106; reliance upon the South, 139; and five-per-cent plurality elections, 152

Depression of 1929, effect on politics, 39-41

De Tocqueville, 2

Dollivor, J. P., 79

Doran, L. A., vii

East, defined, 9, 10; popular votes and population, 45; and Republican success, 45; tariff policy, 45; union with Middle West, 46, 47; and commercial interest, 47; Democratic strength in Connecticut, New York, and New Jersey, 47; Republican votes, 48n.; Democratic votes, 48n.; rejection of Bryan program, 49, 50; election of 1912, 52; rise of Democratic prestige, 54; and Prohibition party, 118; in electoral college, 145-47, 150; five-per-cent elections, 152, 153; effectiveness in electoral college, 172, 173; wastage of popular votes, 178-81; voter participation in, 203, 204

Election of 1876, importance of, 21; loss of Republican prestige in South, 66, 67

Election of 1884, rôle of New York, 136

Election of 1892, results in Middle West, 74

Election of 1896, results in Middle West, 76; in West, 93

Election of 1904, tremendous change in the West, 94, 95

Election of 1912, in East, 52; in Middle West, 79, 80; in West, 95, 96

Election of 1924, in Middle West, 82, 83; in West, 98, 99

Election of 1928, issues in, 37-39; in South, 69-71

Electoral College, votes by parties, 138; and state pluralities, 136, 137, 139-43; quotients, 142-45; New England in, 145, 146; Middle West in, 148-50; West in, 149, 150; South in, 148, 150; Border in, 147, 148, 150; East in, 145-47, 150; sectional distribution of party winners, 165-67, sectional wastage of electoral votes, 167-75

Electoral Commission of 1877, 22

Five-per-cent elections, in East, 152, 153; in Border, 153, 154; in South, 154; in Middle West, 154, 155; in West, 155, 156

Fusion, in South, 67, 68; in Middle West, 75; and the West, 92, 93

222

INDEX

Garfield, James A., election, 23
Garner, John N., 40
George, Henry, 6
Georgia, 9
Godkin, E. L., 25
Graham, Frank P., 68
Grant, U. S., 19; loss of Republican numbers, 20, 21; support of in West, 90
Graph, *see* List of Illustrations, xiii
Greeley, Horace, and Liberal Republican ticket, 19
Greenback Party, 26

Hanna, Mark, 197
Harding, Warren G., 34, 35, 98
Harrison, Benjamin, election, 24; support in West, 91
Hayes, Rutherford B., election, 21, 22
Haworth, Paul L., cited, 22
Hicks, John D., quoted, 134, 135
Holcomb, A. N., 9
Hoover, Herbert, stampede to, 17; and reform, 37; and the depression, 39, 40; popularity in Middle West, 84; popularity in West, 100; 101
Hughes, C. E., 97
Hunt, Gaillard, 1

Ickes, Harold L., 18
Indiana, 9
Industrial order, rise of, 5
Industrial reform parties, 121, 122
Industrialism, corporate, and agrarian democracy, 25, 26; and the Middle West, 75; effect on political allegiance 190-92; effect on suffrage increase, 196-98
Interstate Commerce Commission, created, 6
Interventionism, 25-29; 42-44; growth in Middle West after 1900, 77-79; reasons for, 213, 214
Iowa, 11

Jackson, Andrew, revolt against the East, 46

Jefferson, claimed by all parties, 7
Johnson, Hiram, 34, 95, 97, 98

Kansas, 11
Kentucky, 10, 11
Knights of Labor, 26
Know-nothing Party, 131

LaFollette, Robert M., 30, 35, 36, 37, 79; 1924 race in Middle West, 82, 83; popularity in West, 99; 100; votes in East, 113n., 116
Laissez-faire economics, 42-44
Landon, Alfred M., 85, 101, 102
Lincoln, Abraham, challenge by, 3; elected, 4; a Republican saint, 7; re-election, 19; and Dred Scott decision, 72
Looking Backward, 6
Lowden, Frank, 34

McAdoo, William G., 35, 83
McClellan, G. B., votes in Kentucky, Delaware and New Jersey, 19n.
McKinley, William B., 28, 29
Maine, Republican record of, 55
Maryland, 10
Mason and Dixon's Line, 10
Middle West, definition of, 11; union with East, 46, 47; and agrarian democracy, 72, 73; popular votes, 73n.; and industrialism, 75; attitude toward fusion, 75; and election of 1896, 76; reaction to Parker, 76-79; and election of 1912, 79, 80; and pacifism, 81, 82; and agrarian parties, 116; and Prohibition party, 120; in electoral college, 148-50; five-per-cent elections, 154, 155; efficacy in electoral college, 166-69; wastage of popular votes, 178, 183, 184; voter participation in, 204, 205
Minor parties, in Middle West, 74; and education of electorate, 108, 109; rôle of, 108-11; more permanent ones, 110; classification of, 111; popularity in individual states, 128; sectional marks

223

of, 129; future prospects of, 130, 131; contributions of, 131-35; influence in election results, 137

Minnesota, 11; in election of 1912, 136

Missouri, 10

Morris, Frank, viii

Mugwumps, 18, 23

National Politics, 13

Natural Law, 4

Nebraska, 11

New Jersey, 9

Neutrality, and Middle West in 1916, 80

New Deal, and West, 101, 102

New England, states, 9; in electoral college, 145, 146

New York, in election of 1884, 9; 136

Non-Majority elections, 162-65; sectional distribution of party winners, 163n.

Norris, George, 18, 30, 35; on electoral college, 139

North Carolina, 3, 10

Northwest, 11

Ohio, 9; in election of 1892, 136

Oklahoma, and Confederacy, 11; and Socialist strength, 124

Opposition party, rôle of, 8

Pacifism, and Middle West, 81, 82

Parker, Alton B., nominated, 29; unpopularity in Middle West, 76-79; snubbed by West, 94, 95

Party allegiance, before the World War, 16, 17; before 1896, 18; 44

Patriotism, in West, 89

Pennsylvania, 9

Plurality elections, five-per-cent, 151-56

Political party, definition, 7; relation to future, 7, 8

Polk, James K., 133

Popular votes, increase, 14; wastage by periods and sections, 178-88; effective by states, 211, 212

Population, and popular votes, 194-201; and adults, 198-200

Populist party, rise of, 26; fusion with Democrats, 26, 27; unpopularity of fusion in Border, 58, 59; rise in West, 92, 93

Progress and Poverty, 6

Progressivism, in nineteenth century, 27, 28

Prohibition party, 26; the experiment of, 33; in East, 118; in Border, 118, 119; popular votes, 119; in South, 119, 120; in Middle West, 120; in West, 120, 121

Railroads, regulation of, 5; influence of in West, 89, 90

Randolph, John, 131

Reconstruction, comment on, 20

Republican party, formation of, 4; national triumphs, 14; growth of, 15; tariff program, 45, 46; rise of popularity in Border, 61, 62; votes in South in 1928, 70, 71; early strength in Middle West, 73, 74; 1904 gain in Middle West, 76-79, in Middle West, 86, 87; loss of the West in 1896, 93; state percentages of popular votes, 104, 105; split of 1912, 139; loss of popular votes in Middle West in 1932, 140, 141; and five-per-cent plurality elections, 152

Rice, 3

Robinson, E. E., 13, 110 fn.

Roosevelt, Franklin D., and economic security, 18; 34, 40, 41; sweep of Middle West, 84-86; popularity in West, 100-102

Roosevelt, Theodore, and interventionism, 29-31; popularity of in West, 94; 98

Schurz, Carl, 23, 25

Secession, and agrarian democracy, 4; 64, 65

Sections, geographic, criteria of, 9; electoral college votes, 150, 151;

INDEX

percentages of electoral vote effectiveness, 170; relation to national averages of voter participation, 210

Silver, influence of on politics of West, 90, 91

Slavery, and plantation system, 3

Slavocracy, abandonment of Constitution, 4

Smith, Alfred E., 35, 38; unpopularity in South, 69-71; 83, 84; and the West, 100

Socialism, and Populism, 124, 125

Socialists, 27

Socialist party, 122-26; state votes for, 124

"Solid South," emergence of, 67

South, 3; definition, 11; the losing struggle after 1820, 64, 65; effect of Civil War on party allegiance, 65; popular votes, 65n.; crisis in Democratic party in 1892, 67, 68; reaction to Governor Smith, 69-71; agrarian crusades, 114, 115; and Prohibition party, 119, 120; in electoral college, 148, 150; five-per-cent elections, 154; effectiveness in electoral college, 173-75; wastage of popular votes, 178, 182, 183; voter participation in, 200-203

Splinter parties, *see* Minor parties

Stanwood, Edward, 13

States, effectiveness in electoral college, 175-78; effectiveness of popular votes since 1920, 192, 193; effectiveness of popular votes since 1864, 193, 194; records of each in voter participation, 206, 207; effective popular vote, records, 211, 212

Stock market crash of 1929, effect of on parties, 15, 16

Suffrage, restrictions, in South, 68; effect of increase, 75; restriction, effect of in South on minor parties, 115, 116; effect of industrial rise on, 196-98; influence of increased adult population on, 198-200

Taft, William H., 30

Tennessee, 3, 10

Ten-per-cent elections, 156-62; importance of, 156-58; sectional distribution of party winners, 160-62

Third parties, *see* Minor parties

Thompson, "Big Bill," 81

Tilden, Samuel, popular vote in 1876, 137

Tobacco, 3

Tompkins, June, viii

Townsend, plan, 6

United Labor party, 26

Veblen, Thorsten, cited, 49

Vermont, 9; Republican record, 55

Versailles, Treaty of, and effect on American politics, 32, 33

Virginia, 3, 10

Voter participation, relation of to democracy, 194, 195, 201-203; 198-214

Wall Street, 5; Populist abomination of, 216

Wallace, Henry J., 18

Washington, George, 7

Watson, Thomas, 26

Weaver, James B., candidacy in 1880, 23

West, defined, 12; importance of, 87, 88; and faith in democracy, 88-90; and silver policy, 90, 91; refusal to support Cleveland, 91; votes from 1888 to 1908, 91n.; opposition to Wall Street, 92; and fusion, 92, 93; in election of 1916, 97; and 1924 election, 98, 99; total votes, 102, 103; and agrarian parties, 116, 117; and Prohibition party, 120, 121; in electoral college, 149, 150; five-per-cent elections, 155, 156; efficacy in electoral college, 169-71; wastage of popular votes, 178, 184-86; voter participation, 204-08

West Virginia, 10

Wheeler, Burton K., 36, 82

Whig Almanac, 13

Whigs, wrecked, 4; and slavery, 15; 131

Wilson, Woodrow, and the West, 12;

225

and reform legislation, 31; election of, 31; 1912 votes in West, 96; 98
Woman Suffrage, effect of, 14; effect on voter participation ratios of individual states, 208, 209
Wood, Leonard, 34
Woodin, William, 18
World Almanac, viii, 13